Taste Portugal
101

easy Portuguese recipes

from the creators of

Tia Maria's Portuguese Food Blog

Maria Dias and Lisa Dias

Copyright © November 2014

By: Maria Dias and Lisa Dias

dedication

For my husband Augie

my sons Daniel and Christopher

my daughter Lisa

In loving memory of my son Michael

obrigado

Many people in my life have encouraged and inspired me to write my first cook book.

I want to give special thanks to my husband Augie, my sons Daniel and Christopher and my daughter Lisa for their unending love.

To my angel Michael who watches over me.

To my daughter Lisa for helping write this book.

Thank you to my son Christopher for his help with my blog and with this book.

Special thanks to my mother for teaching me how to cook and to share love through food. I also thank her for her strength and faith which has inspired me all of my life.

Thank you to my father who taught me to always reach for success in life.

To my wonderful sisters; Rose and Isabel who have always been my best friends.

Thank you to my brothers for their love, and sharing some great recipes with me.

To my Godmother, who inspired me, to learn how to cook.

To all of my friends and fans from all around the world, I thank them for inspiring me to keep sharing recipes and to write this cook book.

A special thanks to Miguel Carvalho and Carolina Matos for their support, encouragement, and their help in writing this book.

table of contents

appetizers | aperitivos | 32

bread | pão | 63

side dish | acompanhamento | 78

main dish | prato principal | 91

introduction

Food has always been a central part of hosting social gatherings in Portuguese culture which creates a welcoming atmosphere, making even a stranger feel like family. Many of us have fond memories of these moments and the Portuguese dishes shared by our family and friends.

I grew up in a large loving family of Portuguese Immigrants living in America where Portuguese food, culture and tradition played a major role in our daily lives, at every family celebration and during the holidays. Through the years, I've honored these traditions by preparing classic recipes for my own family and friends that were passed down from my ancestors.

I cherish the memories revolving around these dishes which inspired me to create Tia Maria's Blog. With the help and encouragement from my daughter Lisa, we began our labor of love by sharing our recipes. Naming the site, "Tia Maria's Blog" meaning "Aunt Maria's Blog", was inspired from the fact that I have over 30 nieces and nephews who refer to me as "Tia Maria." Most Portuguese families also have a "Tia Maria" of their own which makes the name very familiar and memorable in our culture.

Many people of Portuguese decent living in countries around the world have contacted me for help in finding long lost recipes that were forgotten or never passed down to them by their family members. It's been a very rewarding experience finding many of those lost recipes and the process has been a true inspiration for me to write this cook book.

What began as simply sharing recipes on my blog, has now transformed into a commitment of preserving the rich Portuguese food culture, promoting the nations cuisine, and inspiring people to learn how to cook these recipes so they can pass them on to the next generation.

The recipes contained in this cookbook are easy for the everyday home cook to prepare, they're made with simple ingredients, and they require basic equipment that most home cooks have in their kitchen. Come along, let Lisa and I show you how to cook 101 easy Portuguese recipes, so you can taste Portugal, and create special family memories.

my story

My family originates from a small rural village called Travasos da Cha in the northeastern region of Trás os Montes, mainland Portugal near the border with the Galicia region of Spain. I was born in the city of Braga, in Northern Portugal, during the years in which my parents owned a small restaurant there. To support their family, my parents also farmed potatoes and ran a small bed and breakfast where Spanish peddlers often spent the night and enjoyed my mother's great dishes and our homemade wine.

I migrated to America in 1963, with my parents and five siblings when I was 6 years old. We settled in the charming small New England town of Ludlow, Massachusetts, referred to as "Little Portugal", for its thriving Portuguese community rich in culture and traditions passed on from generation to generation. Portuguese food takes center stage in the community with its many butcher shops offering traditional foods and imported specialty items, bakeries selling classic breads and sweet desserts, and numerous restaurants serving authentic Portuguese dishes on its menu. Growing up with all of the flavors and tastes of Portugal eventually evolved into my passion for its food. My interest in learning to cook first began when I was a young girl often sent to help my Godmother, Tia Alzira, prepare her delicious recipes for the Holidays. Before moving to America, Alzira had been a personal Chef to a General in the Portuguese Military, and I was very fascinated by her cooking skills which inspired me to learn how to cook.

My twenty five year career in the food industry began when I was a teenager while working as a waitress for many Portuguese caterers in my hometown. After marrying my high school sweetheart and becoming a mother, I focused my cooking on preparing healthy Portuguese meals for my family. For over 10 years I was employed at a Portuguese American restaurant which my brothers owned called, The Matador. My cooking skills evolved at the restaurant where I learned different cooking techniques and classic recipes from the professional Portuguese chefs who were employed there.

A few years later, after the restaurant was sold, my husband and I decided to open a small hometown restaurant called; The Hometown Deli, where I was the cook and manager. I cooked many homemade dishes and thousands of homemade soups there, and to this day my family still refers to me as their; "Soup Queen"! My cooking skills continued to evolve through the years. I became the Chef/Manager of a gourmet coffee shop/restaurant called Nancy's Coffee Café, where I developed my knowledge about gourmet foods, and coffees from countries around the world.

Today, I am no longer working in the food industry, but cooking Portuguese food remains my passion. I enjoy preparing classic dishes with my daughter Lisa and we devote our free time to sharing these recipes on Tia Maria's Blog.

My Godmother may have been the inspiration for me learning how to cook, so many years ago, but it was my Mother Carmelina who taught me how to cook her recipes with love and to share that love with food. She always had a pot of fresh soup simmering on the stove just in case one of her children or grandchildren stopped by to visit.

My parent's happiest moments were spent with their children and grandchildren during our large family gatherings, celebrations and Holidays where our family's Portuguese recipes were prepared and served.

They are no longer with us, but those moments are fondly remembered and treasured by my brothers, sisters and I, as well as our own families. I honor those same traditions today, by cooking these recipes for my own family and creating our own cherished memories. Thank you Mae for teaching me that family, love, and sharing love with food is what life is all about!

Maria Dias

portuguese cuisine

We could spend many chapters in this book on the history of Portuguese cuisine but that's not what this cookbook is about. Let me share with you a little bit of information and history of Portuguese cuisine.

Portuguese cuisine is a simple and healthy Mediterranean style diet which consists of fresh fish and seafood harvested from the Atlantic seacoast, fresh meats, fruits and vegetables, cheese, wine, olive oil, and egg rich desserts.

The flavors of traditional Portuguese cuisine have evolved through the centuries with the influences from the Romans as well as the Moors who inhabited the region for many centuries. Through the centuries the cuisine continued to evolve with the country's colonization of many countries in the Far East and Africa. Spices such as paprika, coriander, cinnamon, pepper, ginger, curry, saffron and spicy red pepper sauces have enhanced the flavor of the food.

The country of Portugal however, deserves recognition and culinary notoriety as having influenced the cuisine of many nations around the world. Since the Portuguese explorers sailed the seas in the 15th century in quest of an ocean route to the East in search of spices, their journey introduced the world to many spices and wines, citrus fruits, potatoes, corn, chili and even coffee to the Americas and Brazil.

If you love Shrimp Tempura, you can thank the explorers that introduced the frying technique to Japan. Chili was first created in India due to the Portuguese long red peppers being brought to the land of Goa. The traditional "Tea Time" in England became popular due to King Charles II marring the Portuguese Princess Catherine de Braganza whose dowry included Far East tea trading routes.

Portuguese immigrants who settled in many nations all around the world have also inspired the cuisine of their host nations. The flavors and tastes of Portugal can be found in countries from as far away as Macau, to Australia, and to the United States and Canada.

In the New England coastal ports where Portuguese fisherman settled to work in the whaling industry, to the State of California you'll find Portuguese cuisine on many restaurant menus. Hawaiian cuisine has also been influenced by the immigrants that settled there to work in the sugar cane industry. Their famous Malasadas donuts and sweet breads are sold in many bakeries and even McDonald restaurants feature a chouriço and egg breakfast sandwiches on its menu. These are only a few examples of the many culinary influences in many countries around the world by the Portuguese.

Through the years, the classic dishes in Portuguese cuisine may have evolved into a more modernistic form with the talents of world renowned Portuguese chefs, but the true flavors of the ingredients used in the dishes remain.

I predict that eventually the cuisine will be finally recognized and achieve much notoriety in the culinary world that it deserves because the food of Portugal is uniquely appealing, and memorable to anyone who tastes Portugal for the first time.

Come along, let's taste Portugal!

soups | sopas

1 Collard Green Soup

Caldo Verde

Let's begin the first recipe with the classic comforting soup "Caldo Verde" the most loved and popular soup in Portuguese cuisine, which originates from the lush green farmlands of the Northern Minho Region of Portugal where I was born.

The soup is made with basic ingredients of potato and onion puree, collard greens, rich olive oil, and enhanced with the smoky paprika flavored chouriço sausage. It's featured on most menus of Portuguese restaurants and served at weddings and special events. My mother's strong hands taught me how to chiffonade the collard greens into tiny shreds and add them to the soup during the last 5 minutes of cooking time, so they retain their beautiful green color. **Serves: 8-10**

10 Russet or any non-starchy potato

6 cups chicken or vegetable broth

6 cups water

2 large onions

2 cloves garlic

1 large bay leaf

¼ cup olive oil or more to taste

1 tablespoon salt

½ teaspoon pepper

1 whole medium size chouriço (rinsed)

6 cups of washed collard greens (chiffonade very thin)

Place the water, broth, potatoes, onions, garlic, olive oil, and bay leaf in a large soup stock pot. Cook on high heat for 20 to 30 minutes until the potatoes are fully cooked.

Remove from heat and remove bay leaf. Puree the soup with a hand immersion blender until it forms a creamy consistency.

Wash the chouriço and pierce with a fork, and add it to the soup. Cook for about 10 minutes. Remove chouriço and slice into ¼ inch slices to be used as a garnish later.

Add the collard greens to the soup and cook only 5 to 8 minutes before serving. Cook longer to your taste if desired.

When ready to serve the soup, place 3 slices of the reserved chouriço into each bowl for garnish. Add a drizzle of olive oil over the soup and crushed black pepper to taste.

Note:

You may cook the chouriço in a separate pan of boiling water if you don't want a smoky flavored soup.

My recipe is for a large pot of soup that will last for a few days in the refrigerator.

If you find that it has thickened the next day, just add a little amount of boiling water to create a thinner broth.

2 Kale and Chouriço Soup
Sopa de Couve com Chouriço

Kale Soup is very popular in our cuisine, but it is often mistaken for Caldo Verde soup. This recipe is an Azorean version which uses chunky potatoes and chopped kale rather than a potato puree. This soup has sliced chouriço sausage, chunky potatoes, crushed ripe tomatoes and chopped kale.

There are many variations of this recipe. Some cooks add red, white beans, root vegetables, chick peas, or even pasta. If you prefer a thicker style broth let the soup cook for at least one hour on simmer for the vegetables to dissolve creating a thicker soup.

Serves 6-8

3 potatoes (peeled and chopped into 1 inch cubes)

4 cups chicken broth

2 cups water or more

3 to 4 cups kale (chopped)

2 tablespoons olive oil

1 large onion (chopped)

2 cloves garlic (chopped)

1 bay leaf

1 (32 oz.) can red kidney beans

1 teaspoon salt

½ tsp pepper

Olive oil for garnish

1 (16 oz). can diced tomatoes

1 medium chouriço or linguica sausage (sliced ¼ inch thick)

In a large soup pot, cook onions and chouriço in the olive oil for a few minutes until onion is translucent.

Add the broth, water, potatoes, garlic, bay leave, and kale. Cook for about 5 minutes.

Add the, beans, tomatoes, and bring to a boil.

Cover, reduce heat to low and continue cooking until the potatoes are tender for an additional 15 to 20 minutes.

Serve with a drizzle of olive oil on top.

Note:

You may substitute white beans or chick peas for the kidney beans if you prefer.

Add more boiling water to thin out broth to your preference.

Cook longer if you prefer a thicker broth.

3 Butternut Squash and Spinach Soup
Sopa de Abóbora e Espinafres

This healthy soup has a butternut squash and carrot puree base which makes a rich and flavorful broth. You may substitute the spinach with any leafy green cabbage but be sure to cook the greens longer to your desired taste. **Serves 6-8**

2 cups butternut squash (chopped)

2 large carrots (chopped)

8 cups water

1 large onion

1 scallion (optional)

¼ cup olive oil

1 teaspoon salt

¼ teaspoon pepper

2 chicken bouillon cubes

2 cups baby spinach

Cook all of the ingredients with the water except the spinach and butter in a medium soup pan until the vegetables are tender.

Remove the pan from the burner and add the butter.

Puree the vegetables with an immersion blender until smooth and creamy.

Place the soup back on the burner on low heat and simmer for about 5 minutes.

Wash the spinach and add to the soup. Cook the spinach for only 5 minutes or more depending on your taste.

Serve with crushed black pepper if desired.

4 Shrimp Vegetable Bisque

Caldo de Camarão

This shrimp lovers soup is filled with shrimp flavor and tangy spices. The rich broth is made using whole shrimp including the heads and shells which brings out the rich shrimp flavor.

I learned this recipe many years ago from a Portuguese chef named José who worked at my brother's Portuguese restaurant. He was a great chef, but very temperamental in the kitchen. His mood swings were evident by the loud echoes coming from the pots and pans that were often thrown around in the kitchen. **Serves 8-10**

2 pounds raw shrimp (30 to 40) per pound (head on if available)

1 large onion (chopped)

1 large garlic clove

4 large carrots (peeled and chopped)

2 stacks of celery (peeled and chopped)

8 cups water

2 tablespoons olive oil

2 shrimp bouillon cubes

2 tablespoons butter

1 teaspoon paprika

1 or 2 teaspoons salt (depending on your taste)

1 teaspoon white pepper

1 to 2 teaspoons of piri piri or Tabasco sauce

½ cup Vinho Verde or white wine

½ cup cream (optional)

3 Portuguese rolls to make croutons

Lemon wedges for garnish

Chopped parsley or cilantro for garnish

Peel and devein the shrimp and reserve the shells and heads. Rinse the shells and put the shrimp meat aside.

In a large stock pot, add the 8 cups of water, the shrimp shells and heads, ½ of the onion, garlic, celery, carrots, salt, and pepper, and cook for 30 minutes.

Strain the broth, and throw away the shells. Place the carrots, onions and celery back into the broth. Look for any small pieces of shell and remove them.

Puree the soup with a hand blender until the soup reaches a creamy base. Strain the soup through a fine strainer to catch any shells, or vegetable threads. Place the soup back on the stove on low heat.

Meanwhile, in a medium skillet, saute the remaining onion in the olive oil and butter until translucent.

Add the shrimp, the bouillon, wine, paprika, and piri piri. Cook for a few minutes until the shrimp is pink. Remove ½ of the cooked shrimp and set aside.

Add the remaining shrimp and onion sauce to the soup pan and puree to a creamy consistency. Cook the soup on low heat for 10 minutes.

Cut the reserved cooked shrimp in half and add to the soup. Cook on low heat for 5 minutes.

Taste the soup and add more salt and white pepper to taste.

Make the croutons:

Slice the Portuguese rolls into small ¼ inch slices. Coat with butter and garlic and toast until golden brown in the oven or in a toaster. Set aside for garnish.

Serve Soup:

When ready to serve, place in bowls with a few pieces of shrimp halves and one slice of the toasted Portuguese croutons in the center.

Add the cilantro or parsley as garnish if desired. Squeeze a little lemon into the soup if desired.

Note:

If you like a creamier soup, simply add a little heavy cream.

Always save your leftover shrimp shells from your recipes to make shrimp stocks. Rinse the shells, pat dry and place them into freezer bags

5 Portuguese Seafood Chowder
Sopa de Marisco

Portugal was known as Lusitania by the Romans, and was highly prized for its seafood harvested along the coast and then shipped to Rome. Today, the Portuguese population is among the world's largest per capita fish consumers. **Serves 8-10**

1 large onion (diced)

¼ cup olive oil

1 pound potatoes (peeled and chopped into 2 inch cubes)

1 pound shrimp (shell on)

8 little neck clams

1 pound scallops

1 fresh lobster cut into pieces

1 pound cleaned squid (chopped)

1 tablespoon tomato paste

1 small pepper (diced)

4 cups fish stock or clam juice

2 cups water

½ cup white wine

1 bay leaf

¼ cup crushed tomatoes

1 teaspoon paprika

Salt and pepper to taste

Chopped cilantro or parsley (garnish)

¼ teaspoon crushed red pepper (optional)

Preparation:

In a large pan, sauté the onion with the olive oil until translucent.

Add the lobster, tomatoes, paprika, bay leaf, and wine, and saute for a few minutes until slightly brown.

Add the potatoes, wine, water, broth, bell pepper, tomato paste, and spices and cook for about 15 minutes on medium heat.

Add the clams, shrimp, mussels and calamari, and cook until all the clams and mussels open, which should be about 10 to 15 minutes.

Add crushed red pepper flakes if desired.

Garnish with cilantro or parsley.
Serve with crusty bread.

6 Savoy Cabbage Vegetable Soup
Sopa Juliana

Cabbage is a staple in Portuguese cuisine and often served in soups or as a side dish served with a drizzle of olive oil and vinegar. This simple soup is easy to make and very versatile since you can use any type of broth such as chicken, beef or even vegetable. For a more meaty flavored soup, cook a ham or beef bone along with the vegetables for at least one hour. **Serves 8-10**

4 cups savoy or regular cabbage sliced into 1 inch strips

2 large potatoes

4 carrots

4 cups water

4 cups beef, chicken or vegetable broth

½ cup rice or pasta

1 large onion

1 clove garlic

3 tablespoon olive oil

1 teaspoon salt

1 teaspoon pepper

Crushed red pepper flakes (optional)

Place the water, and broth, carrots, potatoes, onions, garlic, salt, and 1 cup of the cabbage in a large soup pan.

Let it come to a boil and cook on medium heat for 30 minutes. (Cook for at least 1 hour if you add a soup bone.)

When the vegetables are cooked, puree the soup with an immersion blender to your desired consistency.

Add the remaining cabbage, rice, or pasta and olive oil, and cook for an additional 20 minutes on low heat.

Add fresh cracked pepper and crushed red pepper if desired before serving.

Drizzle with a little olive oil in the bowl before serving if desired.

Note:

You may add more water if you find the soup has thickened upon reheating.

7 Green Bean Vegetable Soup
Sopa de Feijão Verde

Heirloom Portuguese flat green beans create this hearty soup. Many families in the Portuguese community grow these beans in their vegetable gardens and save the dried bean seeds to plant the next season. If you don't have these green beans available, you can substitute them with Italian flat green beans from the frozen vegetable isle in your supermarket. Once you try these green beans, you'll never go back to the standard green beans in your recipes again. **Serves: 8-10**

1 large onion (chopped)

3 large carrots (chopped)

1 large clove garlic

3 tablespoons olive oil

1 large bay leaf

1 can white northern beans

2 cups fresh flat green beans or 1 (9 oz. box Italian frozen green beans)

2 cups chicken broth or (vegetable if you prefer)

6 cups water

1 tablespoon salt

1 teaspoon pepper

1 tablespoon of any tomato sauce

2 cups small pasta

In a large soup pan, sauté the onions, and carrots in olive oil until translucent. Add the chicken broth, garlic, water, bay leaf, tomato, and seasonings.

Bring to boil and cook on medium heat until vegetables are tender. Remove pan from heat. Remove the bay leaf and add ½ of the can of white beans.

Puree the soup with an immersion blender to desired consistency. Place the soup back on the stove on medium heat. When it comes back up to a boil, add the pasta, green beans, and remaining white beans.

Cover and let it simmer on medium heat for about 15 to 20 minutes until pasta is cooked.

Note:

You may substitute the tomato sauce with a small ripe tomato.

You may also substitute with any type of green beans.

8 White Bean Soup
Sopa de Feijão Branco

Many varieties of beans are used in Portuguese dishes and often used as a staple in many soups and stews. This soup uses white beans and vegetables cooked in a flavorful meat broth. You may substitute the white beans with red kidney beans or chick peas for a different variation on this recipe. **Serves 8 - 10**

8 to 10 cups water

1 ham bone or beef short ribs (optional)

1 large onion (chopped)

1 teaspoon black pepper

¼ cup olive oil

4 or 6 ounces of elbow macaroni

1 (16 oz.). can white northern beans

2 cups savoy cabbage (finely chopped)

1 bay leaf

1 tablespoon salt

2 cloves garlic1 large carrot (chopped)

1 large potato (cubed)

Place all ingredients except the macaroni, beans, and cabbage in a large stock pot. Cook on med-high heat for about 1hour. Remove from heat.

Remove bay leaf, and meat bone. Puree all the ingredients with an immersion blender to your desired consistency.

Place soup back on stove, let it simmer for about 5 minutes and bring to a boil. Add the macaroni, cabbage, and beans and let soup cook for 10 to 15 minutes.

If you prefer, take the meat off the bone, chop it into small pieces and place into the soup.

Continue cooking the soup until the cabbage is tender.

Serve with crusty bread.

9 Carmelina's Chicken Soup
Canja de Galinha à Carmelina

My mother made chicken soup at least once a week for our family. She always had a pot of soup on the stove just in case a friend or family member stopped by to visit her. There are many recipe variations for chicken soup in every Portuguese kitchen. Some cooks prefer to use rice instead of pasta, while others use small pasta shapes or even egg noodles as the starch. It is also common to add a mint leaf or a squeeze of lemon for added flavor.

Serves: 8-10

2 pounds fresh chicken (whole or cut into pieces)

1 large onion (chopped)

12 cups water

2 large carrots

2 large celery stalks

2 cloves garlic (peeled)

2 sprigs parsley

1 tablespoon salt

½ teaspoon fresh cracked pepper

1 ½ cups Orzo pasta or white rice

2 chicken bouillon cubes

2 teaspoons fresh chopped parsley

Crushed red pepper flakes, mint leaf, squeeze of lemon (optional garnish)

In a large stock pot, place the water, onion, 1 stalk of celery, 1 carrot, salt, 2 sprigs parsley and garlic. Bring to a boil, add the chicken and let it cook on simmer.

After 30 min of cooking, remove chicken breasts from the pot, remove the bones and dice into small chunks. Reserve for later.

Cook for another hour, and remove the chicken and vegetables. Strain the soup through a strainer to remove fats.

Place the soup on the stove and bring to a low boil. Add the Orzo or rice and cook on medium for 10 minutes.

Slice remaining carrot and celery into ¼ inch slices, add to the soup and let it cook for an additional 10 minutes.

Add the reserved diced chicken breast, more salt and pepper, parsley flakes, and let the soup simmer for a few minutes.

Add garnish as desired.

10 Chick Pea Cabbage Soup
Sopa de Grão com Couve

The combination of cabbage and chick peas create a hearty soup that is loaded with protein and fiber. I puree the chick peas for a thicker broth, but if you prefer a chunkier style leave them whole or puree only half of them. This is a perfect fall soup when carrots and cabbage are at their peak of harvest season.

Serves 6-8

2 large carrots (chopped)

1 (16 oz). can cooked chick peas

8 cups water

1 bay leaf

1 large onion

¼ cup olive oil

1 teaspoon salt

¼ teaspoon pepper

2 Chicken bouillon cubes

1 to 2 cups chopped savoy cabbage

Cook all of the ingredients except the cabbage in a medium soup pan on medium high heat until the vegetables are tender.

Remove the pan from the burner and puree the soup with an immersion blender until smooth and creamy.

Place the soup back on the burner on low heat and simmer for about 5 minutes.

Taste the soup and add more water or seasoning if desired. Add more water if you find the soup has thickened too much.

Add the cabbage and cook on low heat for 5 to 10 minutes and serve

Note:

If you like a chunkier style soup, simply puree only one half of the vegetables.

Garnish with fresh cracked black pepper.

appetizers | aperitivos

11 Portuguese Style Spicy Shrimp
Camarão Piri Piri

This is my family's favorite appetizer. We serve it every time we have a family party or celebration. The piri piri red pepper sauce and smoked paprika give these pan grilled shrimp a beautiful color and a spicy kick. I love this dish because it only takes minutes to prepare and you can adapt it to your guest's tastes simply by adding more or less spice.

Be sure to have plenty of Portuguese rolls on hand for dipping into the sauce. A word of warning, the people you make this for will be forever in your life from then on. I promise you. It's that good!

Serves 4-6

2 pounds uncooked shrimp (30 to 40 per pound size, unpeeled and defrosted)

1 very small onion (finely chopped)

3 tablespoons olive oil

1 teaspoon smoked paprika

1 chicken bouillon cube

¼ cup Vinho Verde or very dry white wine

¼ teaspoon salt

1 teaspoon corn starch

2 to 3 teaspoons piri piri or (Tabasco or any hot sauce)

½ cup water

In a large skillet, sauté onions in olive oil on medium heat until translucent but not browned.

Add the shrimp and cook for 1 minute until the shrimp is pink. Add the paprika, salt, bouillon cube, wine and hot sauce. Stir and cook for 1 minute.

Make slurry with ¼ to ½ cup water and corn starch. Mix together in small cup until the corn starch is dissolved. Stir into the shrimp.

Cook until the sauce thickens. Taste the sauce and add more salt or hot sauce to your taste.

Note:

This recipe takes only a few minutes to prepare. Start cooking it just before you're ready to serve it to your guests.

You can also make it ahead of time and heat it up for a few minutes. Do not overcook the shrimp since it may become rubbery if you overcook them.

12 Codfish and Potato Croquettes
Bolinhos de Bacalhau | Pasteis de Bacalhau

There's a saying in Portugal; "There are 365 recipes for bacalhau, one for each day of the year." These little cod fish croquettes are the most popular appetizer in Portuguese cuisine. They are considered a must have at every Christmas table, wedding, and celebration. This is my mother's recipe. I have fond memories of cooking these "bolinhos" with her every Christmas Eve morning. I've adapted the family tradition by making them with Lisa every Christmas Eve. I recommend that you make a double batch and freeze half of the raw batter for the next time. The savory potato and codfish batter is lightly fried until golden brown and they come out spectacularly delicious! **Makes 4-5 dozen**

1 pound boneless bacalhau (salt cod)

3 large non starchy potatoes peeled and cut into ½ inch slices

1 small yellow onion (minced)

1 large garlic clove (very finely minced) or (¼ teaspoon of garlic powder)

2 teaspoons olive oil

2 teaspoons parsley (very finely minced)

3 large beaten eggs

¼ teaspoon crushed black pepper

Salt

Corn oil or vegetable oil for frying (use a top brand not a generic to avoid a greasy taste)

How to Hydrate Cod:
See page 100

Preparation:

Place potatoes, and cod fish in a pan with enough water to cover them. Cook on medium heat at a low rolling boil for about 10 minutes.

Gently remove the codfish which should be flaky and tender with a slotted spoon and place on a clean white linen kitchen towel or paper towels to absorb its moisture.

Remove any pin bones and roll the cod in the towel to form a ball and squeeze out any moisture. Set aside.

Continue cooking the potatoes for another 10 minutes or until fork tender and drain. After draining, leave the potatoes in the same pan, cover and place back on the burner for a few minutes. This will allow any moisture out of the potatoes. When the potatoes and cod are cooled you can begin making the batter.

Prepare Batter:

Run the potatoes through a potato ricer into a large bowl. This will make them very airy and light. If you don't have a ricer, shred with a cheese shredder.

Flake the cod into tiny shreds with a fork or in a food processor until flaky and light.

Add the flaked cod, onion, garlic, parsley, beaten eggs and pepper to the bowl with potatoes and stir to incorporate ingredients.

Your batter should be thick enough to form oval croquettes for frying. If you find it's too soft, simply add more flaked cod or riced potatoes.

Note:

At this point, you may also form them, roll them in a light coating of flour and store them in freezer bags to cook at a later date.

Heat your oil to about 365 to 375 degrees F and begin frying 4 or five at a time for about 2 to 3 minutes until golden brown.

Test the first batch to be sure they are cooked inside. You may have to adjust the heat lower if you find they are turning brown too quickly and not cooking on the inside.

Place on paper towels to absorb any grease.

Serve warm or cold.

Note: If frozen

Fry them while still frozen but it may take longer to cook them through.

Adjust the heat accordingly to cook evenly.

13 Shrimp Empanadas
Rissóis de Camarão

This appetizer is very popular and served at most weddings and special events. The tender dough is filled with shrimp filling and then lightly fried until golden brown, creating a mouthwatering bite that melts in your mouth.

When I was a little girl, I often went to my Godmother's house to help her make dozens of these treats for our family's Christmas Eve dinner called the "Consoada." The word Consoada is a meal that is eaten after a day's fasting and originates from the Latin word consolare, meaning "to comfort" since many people fast during the Advent days before Christmas. The Consoada dinner is bountiful with many fish and seafood dishes as well as many classic desserts.

I was often scolded by my Godmother for breaking open the dough which is very tender and must be handled very gently, both in the forming process and in the frying. Through the years, Lisa and I have acquired the same meticulous care while making them every Christmas Eve. **Makes 5-6 Dozen**

Step 1 White Sauce Preparation:

6 tablespoons flour	In heavy sauce pan melt butter, add flour and stir until it dissolves into the butter.
¾ stick or 6 tablespoons of butter or margarine	Add milk, salt pepper and bouillon cube. Cook on medium heat and constantly stir until it thickens.
2 cups milk	
½ teaspoon salt	In a small bowl, add 1 tablespoon of the prepared white sauce to a beaten yolk to temper, and then add the egg mixture into the white sauce.
¼ teaspoon pepper	
½ of a chicken bouillon cube (optional)	Stir, taste and add more salt or pepper if needed.
1 egg yolk	Set aside to cool or cover with saran wrap in the refrigerator to cool completely.

Step 2 Shrimp Filling Preparation:

¼ cup onion (finely minced)	*Preparation:*
2 teaspoons parsley (finely minced)	Cook the onions in olive oil on medium heat. Add bouillon and shrimp. Cook for about 3 minutes until shrimp is pink.
½ of a chicken bouillon cube	
3 tablespoons olive oil	Add lemon juice and parsley and let cool.
1 ½ pounds raw shrimp (peeled and finely chopped)	Fold the cooled shrimp into the white sauce and season w/ salt and pepper.
¼ teaspoons paprika	Let the mixture cool completely, or store overnight in refrigerator covered with plastic wrap.
1 teaspoon lemon juice	
¼ teaspoons salt (optional)	

Step 3 Dough Preparation:

6 cups water

6 cups flour

1 tablespoon salt

1 stick or 8 tablespoons margarine

1 piece of lemon peel

Preparation:

In heavy nonstick pan, place water, lemon peel, salt and butter on medium heat until the water starts to boil and the butter melts.

Remove the lemon peel. Add the flour and continually stir with a sturdy spoon until a ball of dough forms. This takes muscle power.

You'll notice the bottom of the pan starts to form a crust. Keep stirring until all of flour is absorbed into the ball of dough.

The batter should feel and look like bread dough.

Note:

Let the dough cool completely before rolling to form the empanadas.

Step 4 Forming Empanadas

Once the dough and fillings have completely cooled, roll out dough onto a cold floured surface to 1/8 inch thick with floured rolling pin.

Cut the dough into round 4 to 5 inch circles using a cookie cutter, or a cup with a thin rim.

Place 1 teaspoon of filling in center of dough. Fold the dough over forming a moon shape.

Carefully pinch edges together with a fork. Don't let filling escape out of the sides. If the dough bursts you'll find it's because you added too much filling.

Place the Rissóis apart from each other on a large cookie sheet covered with parchment paper or lightly floured.

Note:

At this point, you can freeze them in plastic bags for up to 1 month.

Step 5 Coating the Empanadas

Beat 3 eggs with a couple tablespoons of water in large bowl and set aside.

Spread 2 to 3 cups fine bread crumbs on a flat tray.

Using one hand dry, one hand wet method, dip each shrimp empanada into the egg wash and then into the bread crumbs.

Shake off excess egg and crumbs and place them onto parchment lined cookie sheets.

Store in refrigerator covered with plastic wrap until ready to fry.

Step 6 Frying Empanadas

Heat a deep fryer to 365 degrees F.

Note:

I recommend a good stainless steel fryer that regulates the heat to 365 degrees.

Fry 6 at a time until golden brown. If they are browning too quickly and raw inside, turn down the heat setting. You may have to adjust the heat accordingly depending on your fryer.

Keep gently turning them over to cook evenly. The dough is very tender, be careful not to pierce the dough or the turnover will burst open and allow grease into the center.

Test one for doneness, by cutting it open to make sure the filling and the dough is cooked through. Place on paper towels to absorb grease.

14 Little Neck Clams à Bulhão Pato Style
Ameijoas à Bulhão Pato

This dish is named after the 19th-century Lisbon poet, Bulhão Pato, and is now featured on most Portuguese restaurant's menus. The fresh cilantro & white wine sauce creates a flavorful broth from the herbs, wine, and tender, juicy clams. Serve with crusty Portuguese home style bread for dipping. **Serves 1-2**

2 tablespoons olive oil

1 tablespoon garlic (diced)

1 tablespoon fresh cilantro (finely chopped)

3 tablespoons Vinho Verde or dry white wine

12 little neck clams (rinsed & cleaned)

Lemon wedges

In a saute pan, cook the garlic in olive oil over high heat until translucent.

Add the clams, white wine, ½ cilantro, and cover.

Cook on low for 5 to 8 minutes until the clams have opened.

Discard any unopened clams.

Place in serving dish.

Top with cilantro and lemon wedges.

15 Codfish Cakes
Pataniscas de Bacalhau

These flat cakes have a savory flavor from the codfish combined with the sweetness from the onions and parsley. You can serve them as appetizers or as a main dish served with rice. They are even better the next day, so go ahead and make a double batch.

I have fond memories of learning how to cook these Pataniscas with my mother when I was a little girl. We would make these on Sunday mornings to bring along on our family day trips or for picnics on the beach.

Makes 10-12 cakes

1 pound boneless salt cod (bacalhau) (minced)

4 eggs

1 and ½ cups flour

½ small onion or scallions (minced)

2 teaspoons fresh parsley (minced)

¼ teaspoon black pepper

¼ teaspoon garlic powder

1 teaspoon olive oil

Salt to taste

½ to 1 cup water

½ teaspoon baking soda

¼ cup olive oil

¼ cup vegetable oil

Cook the cod in boiling water for about 5 to 8 minutes. Let it cool, and then shred it into small flakes with a fork.

In a bowl, mix onion, parsley, cod, flour, salt, pepper, garlic powder and the olive oil, and mix well.

Mix the water and the eggs in a small bowl and add to the bacalhau mix and stir well.

Taste and add more salt, pepper and garlic powder to desired taste.

Combine both oils and begin frying in batches by heating half of the oils to ¼ inch in a heavy skillet on medium heat.

Test the oil temperature by placing a tiny amount of batter in oil. If batter sizzles it's ready to fry in. If you see the oil begin to smoke, lower the heat.

Spoon silver dollar sized pancake batter into pan. Pat them down to cook flat to about ¼ inch oval shapes. Cook until golden brown on each side.

Place them on paper towels or brown paper lunch bags to absorb any grease.

Serve hot or cold.

16 Puff Pastry Beef Pockets
Pasteis de Carne

These puff pastry pockets are filled with a savory meat filling then baked until golden brown. They are delicious warm, but taste even better the next day.

This recipe makes about 3 dozen meat pastries which makes it a great hand held party dish. You can also substitute the beef with cooked chicken for a variation.

Makes approximately 3 dozen

2 pounds frozen or fresh puff pastry dough

1 pound ground beef

¼ cup onion (finely chopped)

1teaspoon garlic powder

2 teaspoon parsley (chopped)

Salt and pepper

¼ cup shredded cheese (optional)

1 egg

1 teaspoon water

Preparation:

Remove the dough from the freezer to defrost it out enough to roll out.

In a large skillet, cook meat until browned. Remove from pan, drain and set aside to cool in a medium bowl.

In same skillet add onions and garlic and cook until golden brown. Add onion mix to meat and let cool.

Place meat mixture in food Processor pulsing 5 times or until the meat reaches a fine consistency. Add parsley and cheese and pulse 2 more times.

Roll out pastry dough and cut into 3″ x 6″ rectangle. Place 1 tablespoon meat in center of rectangle. Fold over one side onto the other to create square pockets while pinching edges.

Cover 2 baking sheets with parchment paper. Place puffs onto the paper and brush with a light egg wash.

Cook in preheated oven at 400 degrees F for 15 minutes or until golden brown.

17 Savory Beef Croquettes
Croquetes de Carne

This croquette recipe is an old classic. They are savory and light and have a crispy outer crust. It's a perfect way to use your leftover roast beef or pot roast.

I made many of these Croquetes when I was a young girl. I would be the official croquette roller whenever I went to my Godmother's house to help her cook them for our Christmas Eve dinner. **Makes 2 dozen**

---

1 pound cooked roast beef (finely minced)

2 tablespoons butter

4 tablespoons flour

½ cup milk

3 cloves garlic (finely chopped)

½ of a small onion (finely chopped)

¼ cup chouriço sausage (finely minced) (optional)

1 bay leaf

1 tablespoon parsley (finely chopped)

1 teaspoon salt

¼ teaspoon paprika

Fresh ground black pepper

Dash of nutmeg

2 eggs

1 or 2 cups fine bread crumbs for coating

Preparation:

Saute the onion, garlic, and bay leaf in butter in a medium skillet until translucent. Add the flour and mix well until the flour is incorporated into the butter. Add the milk a little at a time until the butter is melted and the mixture is smooth and thickened.

Add the beef, chouriço, and all remaining spices and cook for a few minutes. Remove the bay leaf and discard.

Remove the beef from heat and add 1 beaten egg a little at a time to temper it. Cook the mixture until it becomes thick and form into balls or egg shapes. Cool the mixture for a few minutes and shape into croquettes.

When ready to fry, dip each croquettes in the remaining beaten egg and then into bread crumbs. Fry on medium high in vegetable oil until golden brown. Drain onto paper towels before placing them on the serving platter.

18 Portuguese Style Cold Cut Platter
Carnes Frias e Queijos à Portuguesa

This appetizer will tempt your guest's pallet while you prepare dinner or you can serve this as a party dish. To give the dish a rustic look, I serve the cold cuts on a large wooden cutting board. When your guests are finished eating, simply roll up the paper and throw it away for easy clean up.

Cheese:

Azeitão

Évora cheese

Nisa

Pico

São Jorge

Serpa

Serra da Estrela

Cured Meats:

Salpicao

Chouriço

Mortadella

Presunto

Sides:

Variety of olives

Cherry or grape tomatoes

Roasted red peppers

Dried figs or fig jam

Assorted nuts

Sliced breads

Place a large sheet of parchment paper over a large wooden cutting board or a large serving platter.

Arrange olives, tomatoes, peppers, pickles or other condiments in the center.

Surround with various Portuguese cheeses, cured meats.

Add finely sliced crusty bread varieties around the sides.

Place serving forks, cheese slicers or knives, and toothpicks for easy serving.

19 Portuguese Style Bruschetta
Bruschetta à Portuguesa

Portuguese rolls are a perfect vessel for the toppings in this appetizer which create a perfect taste of Portuguese flavor all in one bite. The sweet red onions and roasted red peppers tone down the saltiness in the presunto and is then topped with a drizzle of pure Portuguese olive oil.

Make a double batch because these little mouthwatering treats disappear quickly. Make this appetizer up to a day before you're planning to serve it.

Serves 4-6

3 or 4 papo secos (Portuguese rolls or baguette)

2 medium ripe tomatoes (chopped very finely)

2 slices Presunto (finely diced)

¼ cup finely chopped red onions

¼ cup chopped black olives

¼ cup roasted red pepper (finely chopped)

2 cloves garlic (finely diced)

4 tablespoons Portuguese olive oil or an extra virgin olive oil

2 teaspoon finely chopped parsley

Crushed black pepper to taste

Prepare toppings:

Drain the tomatoes and place them in a plastic or ceramic bowl. Add the remaining ingredients and mix well.
Store in the refrigerator until ready to assemble and serve.

Prepare bread slices:

Place 1 chopped garlic clove in olive oil, in a very small microwave safe bowl and cook for about 30 seconds to infuse the oil with garlic flavor.

Slice the bread into very thin ¼ to ½ inch slices and place each one flat down onto a large baking sheet. Brush with the half of the garlic oil, leaving other half for the topping.

Place tray with the slices of bread under the broiler to toast for about 2 minutes or until a light golden brown turning over to brown the other side.

Caution:

Leave oven door open while toasting bread. It will brown quickly.

When bread is done, place 1 tablespoon or more of the topping mix onto each slice. Drizzle top with olive oil if desired and serve.

20 Grilled Pork Bellies
Toucinho Assado

There's nothing like the smell of fresh pork fat cooking on the outdoor grill. This is my brother Manny's recipe served every time we have a family picnic and a favorite of the men in our family.

You can find non-cured pork belly at your local butcher shop. They will hand slice it to your desired thickness. Be sure to serve it with Portuguese rolls or crusty bread for absorbing the succulent juices from the crispy cooked bacon. **Serves 6-8**

---

2 pounds of fresh non cured pork belly (sliced ¼ inch thick)

6 cloves garlic (chopped)

1 tablespoon sea salt

2 tablespoons olive oil

Marinate the pork strips in the salt garlic and olive oil for at least 30 minutes.

Place on hot grill and cook until both sides are crispy, but not burned.

Serve with crusty Portuguese bread.

21 Pork Cracklings Minho Style
Rijões à Minhota

The word "Minhota" often refers to a female from the region of "Minho" in Northern Portugal where the dish originates from. The garlic and wine marinade creates savory flavorful pork. The braising technique creates a golden and crispy texture. Serve with crusty bread or with boiled potatoes as a main dish. **Serves 4-6**

1 pound pork butt cut into small 1 inch cubes

1 cup Vinho Verde or dry white wine

3 cloves garlic (finely chopped)

1 bay leaf

½ tablespoon paprika

½ teaspoon cumin

½ tablespoon salt

½ teaspoon of crushed black pepper

3 tablespoons shortening

Place all ingredients except the shortening in a small bowl and mix very well to incorporate the spices. Place in the refrigerator to marinate overnight.

When you're ready to cook, remove the meat from the refrigerator to let it reach room temperature. Drain the pork, but save the marinade for later.

In a large skillet, heat the shortening on medium high heat and cook the pork until golden brown and crispy. Cook pork in batches obtaining a nice crispy texture.

Remove the final batch of cooked meat from pan. Add the marinade to the pan and let it cook until it reduces by a half.

Add the pork back into pan and cook for a few minutes to incorporate the flavors. Taste and add more salt if desired.

Serve with crusty bread as an appetizer or you can serve this pork as a main dish with simple boiled potatoes.

22 Portuguese Style Cheese Platter
Queijos Portugueses

This rustic cheese platter is a great way to start off your dinner or for hosting a simple cheese and wine party. I make this very often when I'm entertaining a large crowd for a dinner party because it keeps the guests busy while I finish cooking dinner.

If you're hosting a wine party, serve with Portuguese dry or sweet wines, white, red, Vinho Verde, Port Wine, or Madeira wine combinations.

Variety of Portuguese cheeses:

Azeitão

Évora cheese

Nisa

Pico

São Jorge

Serpa

Serra da Estrela

Condiments:

Almonds

Walnuts

Fig jam

Marmelada (Portuguese Quince Jam)

Variety of sliced breads

Wooden cutting board
or platter

Place almonds, fig jam and Marmelada in the center of cutting board. Arrange various cheeses around the jams.

Place sliced breads and crackers around the cheese.

Serve with Portuguese dry or sweet wines, white, red, Vinho Verde, Port Wine, or Madeira combinations.

23 Red Bean and Chouriço Chili
Chouriço com Feijão

The smoky paprika and spices create a perfect combination of flavors in this chili. It's great for a party, or as a bean side dish for your next cookout. This family favorite which we call Portuguese Chili is my husband Augie's recipe. **Serves 4-6**

---

1 large chouriço or linguica cut into ¼ inch slices.

2 large cans cooked red kidney beans

1 small onion (chopped)

2 medium garlic cloves (chopped)

1 bay leaf

½ teaspoon paprika

1 to 2 teaspoons of piri piri or hot sauce (optional)

½ cup water

½ cup red wine

1 cup crushed red tomatoes or tomato sauce

2 tablespoons olive oil

2 tablespoons parsley flakes (optional)

In a large deep saucepan on medium heat, saute the onions, garlic and bay in the olive oil for 1 to 2 minutes until translucent.

Add the sliced chouriço and let it cook for about 2 minutes until slightly browned.

Add the remaining ingredients except the parsley flakes and let it come to a boil. Reduce heat and simmer on low for 15 to 20 minutes stirring on occasion.

Cover and set aside until ready to serve. The chili will thicken as it cools.

Note:

You will notice the chili may be slightly watery. To thicken, simply mash about 1 cup of the beans with a fork, stir back into the chili and let it cook until it reaches your desired consistency.

To heat up the next day, add a little boiling water to thin out the chili and heat on low stirring often.

24 Broiled Chouriço
Chouriço Bombeiro

This appetizer creates a memorable cooking experience for your guests. The flaming chouriço creates a crispy brown skin and savory flavor. Chourico sausage is cured so don't worry if think you haven't cooked it long enough. Serve with fresh crusty bread.
Serves 4-6

1 Whole linguica or chouriço

2 to 4 oz. whole grain alcohol

1 oven proof deep dish clay cooking vessel or oven proof dish

Long fireplace matches

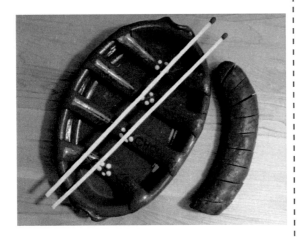

Rinse and dry the chouriço with paper towels.

Place 2 oz. of Alcohol in the bottom of an oven proof dish.

Make a few diagonal cuts into the chouriço and place on cooking dish.

Light a match and slowly light the alcohol. Let the flames cook the chouriço until crispy.

Note:

Caution - do not touch flames. Cook in well-ventilated area.

Turn the chouriço over to cook the other side if desired.

If the flames die out before the chouriço is cooked, start the process over.

Remove the chouriço onto a serving plate and serve in slices.

25 Grilled Sardines with Onions and Peppers
Sardinhas Assadas com Cebolada

Sardines are as popular in Portugal as the infamous bacalhau. Most summer festivals and picnics will feature sardines. Portuguese sardines have the Blue Label awarded by the Marine Stewardship Council, which means fishing of sardines in Portugal takes account of the sustainability of the sea resources. Sardine catches happen all along the Portuguese Coastline but the most favored sardines come from the Algarve region. Portimão in the Algarve is where you eat the best fresh grilled sardines, especially at the Sardine Festival during the first 10 days of August. **Serves 4-6**

2 pounds fresh or frozen sardines

1 large red bell pepper (cut in half)

1 large green bell pepper (cut in half)

2 large onions (sliced into large rings)

2 large garlic cloves (chopped)

¼ to ½ cup extra virgin olive oil

Sea salt

Pepper

How to prepare frozen or fresh sardines for grilling:

If your sardines are frozen, defrost them in a large bowl by first rinsing them with cold water, drain and cover with a good coating of sea salt.

Let them sit at room temperature for about 30 minutes to absorb the salt.

If you're not cooking them right away, drain any moisture from the bowl, cover and set in the refrigerator until you're ready to grill.

If you have fresh sardines coat them with sea salt and let them sit for about 5 minutes before grilling.

Cook Peppers and Onions First:

Heat the grill on high. Rub the onions and peppers with salt, pepper and a little olive oil. Cook the peppers and onions on the grill until the skin is totally charred and then place peppers in a clean paper lunch bag. Put the onions aside for later.

Grilling Sardines:

Remove the sardines from the refrigerator and drain off any liquid.

Pat them dry and place them on a slightly greased charcoal or gas grill on medium high heat.

Let the sardines cook until they turn golden brown and slightly crispy turning them gently with a fork being careful not to break the skin.

Keep the sardines off open flame to avoid getting black char marks.

When they are fully cooked, cover with foil and place them on a platter in a warm oven.

Prepare Peppers and Onions:

Remove the peppers from the paper bag and peel off the skin. You'll find the skin will come out easily. Slice peppers into strips and mix with the onions in a medium skillet.

Add the garlic, olive oil and more salt and pepper. Warm the mixture slightly.

.

Serve:

Place the warm cooked sardines in the center of a large serving platter. Surround with the onions and pepper sauce.

Serve with boiled potatoes or with fresh Portuguese rolls.

26 Garlicky Octopus Salad
Salada de Polvo

This quick appetizer is a great way to use up your leftover cooked octopus. The onion, garlic and parsley mixed with the extra virgin olive oil vinaigrette create a unique flavor in every bite. Serve with crusty bread or rolls. **Serves 2-4**

3 cups cooked octopus (chopped)

1 teaspoon salt

1 teaspoon pepper

½ of a small onion (chopped)

4 cloves garlic (chopped)

2 tablespoon fresh parsley (chopped)

¼ cup extra virgin olive oil

¼ cup white wine vinegar

Place all ingredients in a bowl and mix together.

Let the mixture sit for at least 15 minutes to marinate before serving.

Serve with crusty bread.

Serve or store in refrigerator for up to 3 days.

27 Chickpea and Egg Salad
Salada de Grão

Chick peas and eggs are very popular and often served as a main dish or as a side dish with fish or bacalhau (cod fish). In this recipe, I use pickled vegetables which add a crunchy texture and a tangy bite. **Serves 2-3**

---

2 cans chick peas

6 sliced hard boiled eggs

½ teaspoon salt

½ teaspoon pepper

½ of a small onion (finely chopped)

2 to 3 tablespoon fresh parsley (finely chopped)

½ cup pickled vegetables (finely chopped)

¼ to ½ cup extra virgin olive oil

¼ cup white vinegar

Rinse the chick peas, drain and put into a medium bowl.

Mix in all ingredients except the eggs.

Taste and add more seasonings if desired.

Let the mixture sit for at least 15 minutes to absorb flavors.

Top with sliced eggs and garnish with parsley.

28 Deviled Eggs
Ovos Recheados

The word "devil" in the recipe's name originally referred to the combination of spices, including mustard, with which the eggs are seasoned. I use piri piri hot sauce along with the mustard to give these eggs a spicy edge. **Makes 24**

12 eggs

½ cup mayonnaise

1 teaspoon Dijon mustard

¼ teaspoon salt

¼ teaspoon pepper

½ teaspoon piri piri or any hot sauce (optional)

Paprika for garnish

Place the eggs in a medium sauce pan and cover them with water. Boil for 10 minutes and let sit for a few minutes in pan.

Drain and add enough cold water to cover them in the same pan. Let sit for 5 minutes to cool.

Gently tap the eggs, cracking the shell all around the egg. This will make it easy to peel. Carefully slice the eggs length wise and place on a serving dish.

Remove the yolks and place them in a small bowl. Mix in all the ingredients except the paprika. Taste and add more seasoning if desired.

Scoop ½ tablespoon of the yolk mixture into the sliced egg whites. Garnish with paprika.

Note:

Store in refrigerator for 2 days.

29 Portuguese Style Tuna Salad
Salada de Atum

Canned fish and seafood is extremely popular in our cuisine. Many cities in Portugal have shops and restaurants specifically devoted to selling varieties of canned fish such as sardines, tuna, octopus and squid.

This dish can be served as a main dish with boiled potatoes and hard boiled eggs and then topped with a simple olive oil and vinegar dressing. **Serves 2**

1 can tuna fish in water or olive oil

1 cup grape, cherry or any cut up tomatoes

¼ cup onion or scallions (finely minced)

Dressing:

1 tablespoon olive oil

1 tablespoon white wine vinegar

Salt to taste

Pepper to taste

Parsley flakes

Cut the tomatoes in half or into small bites size pieces and place in a medium bowl.

Drain the tuna and add to the tomatoes.

Place remaining ingredients in a small bowl and stir briskly to incorporate the flavors.

Prepare dressing by missing all ingredients in a small bowl. Mix well.

Pour the dressing over the tuna and tomatoes and stir gently.

Serve on a bed of lettuce, with bread, or with boiled potatoes.

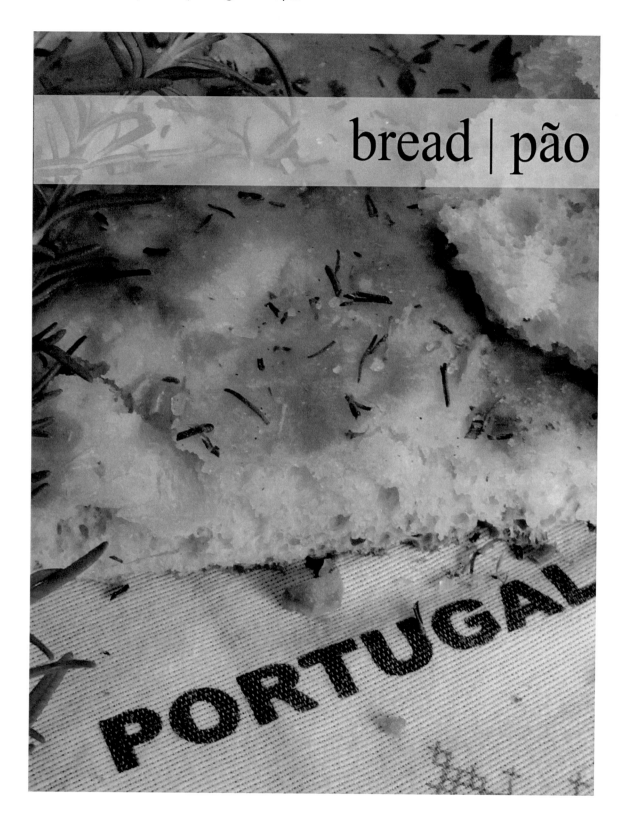

bread | pão

The dog wags his tail, not for you, but for your bread. –Portuguese Proverb

30 Chouriço and Ham Bread Chaves Style
Folar de Chaves

Folar has a long tradition in the culture of Portuguese cuisine. Generally the egg rich bread is stuffed with various cured meats such as; ham, presunto, cured bacon, salpicao and chouriço but there are many variations, and every family has its own recipe. Typically this bread is made during Easter but also very popular all year long.

This "Folar de Chaves" recipe is my mothers. It originated in the north-eastern Portuguese regions of Chaves where she was from. She was famous for her folar and no one was able to replicate it.

Her secret way of kneading the dough by hand until it became light, fluffy and filled with air bubbles, created light and moist bread.

Today, Lisa and I honor my mother's tradition of baking this bread every year during Easter and other family celebrations and holidays. **Makes 2 medium loaves**

---

12 Jumbo brown eggs (room temperature)

10 cups sifted flour

2 (6 oz.) cubes of fresh yeast

1 cup warm water

1 tablespoon salt

1 stick butter or margarine (8 tablespoons)

½ cup olive oil

4 cups smoked ham (ham shank) cut into 1/2 x 2 inch strips

1 or 2 whole – chouriço or linguica sausage (cut into ¼ inch slices)

1 cup chopped (smoked – cured bacon) (if desired)

In a small pan, heat water, margarine and olive oil on low heat. When margarine is melted, test with your finger. It should be warm, not hot.

Add the yeast and stir to dissolve. Set aside. Beat eggs until foamy and set aside.

Sift Flour and salt into a very large mixing bowl. Make a well in the center of the flour and add the eggs and yeast mixture. Knead by hand or with dough hook for at least 10 minutes until dough is light and airy. Look for air bubbles in the batter.

Note:

The batter will be thin and very elastic, not thick like bread dough. If you find it too thin add flour 2 tablespoons at a time and mix well.

Grease your hands with olive oil and shape the dough into a ball. Place the dough in a large bowl that has been greased with olive oil and dusted with flour.

Make a cross in center of the dough to "Bless" it. Cover with plastic and let sit until it has doubled in size about 2 hours.

Note: This step is optional depending on your taste:

Slice the chouriço into desired thickness of slices. Place the meats into a pot of boiling water and let them cook for about 2 to 3 minutes to remove salt. Drain the meats, pat them dry and let them cool. Use meats as is if you prefer saltier bread.

When dough has risen, lightly grease and flour your hands to handle the dough. Pour it onto lightly olive oil greased and floured surface big enough to hold the dough.

Preheat oven to 400 degrees F.

Note: The dough is very tender.

When dough is ready, divide in half. Stretch each piece into a 12 x 16 inch rectangle like handling pizza dough, being careful not to tear it.

Spread the meats evenly over the dough. Begin gently rolling up the dough into a loaf. If any holes form, close them up by pinching the dough together with your fingers.

Place the Folar onto lightly floured sheet pans or into molded bread pans.

Let dough rest for 10 minutes before baking.

Preheat oven to 400 degrees F.

Cook for about 45 minutes at 400 and then lower heat to 350 degrees. Cook another 15 minutes and turn off heat. Cook longer if needed.

The folar should have a dark golden color. Let cool before slicing

Note:

Some ovens may take longer to cook. Check for doneness, by tapping folar with your knuckles. You should hear a hollow sound.

For smaller loaves, cook for 30 to 45 minutes.

Store in the refrigerator.

Note:

You can also freeze the folar by wrapping it in heavy aluminum and then place in freezer bags. It will thaw out a in a few hours or overnight in the refrigerator.

31 Portuguese Sweet Bread
Pão Doce

This light and airy sweet bread is usually made during Christmas and Easter. It's also enjoyed throughout the year for breakfast, during meals, and even served as a dessert. There are many variations of recipes for making this bread, some recipes use raisins, lemon zest, rum or whiskey to intensify the flavor.

Sweet Breads made during Easter are often called Folar de Pascoa where a hardboiled egg is often cooked in the dough to signify fertility and the rebirth of Christ.

Makes approximately 2 large loaves or 24 mini buns

6 to 7 cups flour

2 and ½ packages of active dry yeast

1 cup warm milk

1 stick margarine

1 tablespoon salt

4 jumbo eggs

1 cup sugar

1 tablespoon (whiskey – aguardente) (or zest of one lemon if you want lemony flavored bread)

¼ cup warm water

¼ teaspoon sugar

Heat milk, but do not scald. Remove from heat and stir in margarine until melted. Add sugar, salt and mix. Place in a large bowl to cool.

Meanwhile, make yeast starter by mixing yeast with ¼ cup of warm water and ¼ tsp of sugar. Stir until dissolved and let it rest until you see bubbles activating.

Beat eggs for a few minutes then add to the milk. Add the yeast to the milk along with the whiskey and beat for 2 minutes.

Begin adding the flour 1 cup at a time until it's incorporated. Use your dough hooks or your hands to knead for about 10 minutes.

The batter should be very silky and smooth and slightly sticky. Add more flour if you find the dough sticky.

Remove dough from mixer, place on a floured surface and knead for about 5 minutes until the dough is smooth.

Place the dough into a large floured bowl and cover with plastic wrap and a warm towel. Let it rise in a warm place for 2 to 3 hours or until doubled.

After the dough has doubled, punch it down and let it rise for 30 minutes longer. Place your dough on a floured surface and form your bread either into a braid, loaf or mini buns.

Let the dough rise for another hour.

Preheat oven to 325 degrees F.

Brush tops of the bread with egg wash and bake for 30 minutes. After 30 minutes, turn the heat to 300 degrees and cook for 30 minutes longer until the bread has a golden caramel color.

Note:

If you want to make 2 smaller loaves, cook them for about 45 minutes.

Mini buns cook in less time, approximately 45 minutes.

You may find oven temps will vary, adjust accordingly.

32 Artisan Corn Bread
Broa

This very popular corn bread originated in Portugal's northern region of Tras os Montes. What is unusual about making this bread, is that you initially use scalding hot water to pre-cook the corn flour before you add in the regular flour. This is called pre-gelatinization of the corn meal, similar to cooking polenta.

This bread is a perfect match when served with grilled sardines, cured meats, and Portuguese cheeses. I have fond memories of eating this bread in my hometown in Portugal with presunto from Tras os Montes.

Makes 1 loaf of bread

3 and 3/4 cups white or yellow corn flour (not corn meal)

3 cups all-purpose flour

3 cups boiling water

1 tablespoon melted butter

2 teaspoons sugar

2 teaspoons salt

Yeast Starter:

¼ cup warm water

½ teaspoon sugar

2 teaspoons powdered yeast

1 tablespoon flour

Note:

Make the yeast starter first by combining all ingredients and set aside for a few minutes until yeast bubbles form.

Place the corn flour in a mixing bowl and add the boiling water butter, sugar and salt. Mix well with a dough hook or with your hands if the dough is cool enough to handle. This will start the cooking process of the corn flour.

Let the dough rest for about 10 minutes and then add the regular flour a little at a time.

Add the yeast mix and knead until the dough is smooth and can be shaped into a ball.
Place dough on a floured surface, shape into a ball, place in a greased round pan, and top with a dusting of corn flour.

Let the dough double in size for about 1 hour. You'll notice the cracks forming on the dough but that is what gives the dough an artisan appearance.

Meanwhile preheat oven to 450 degrees F. Cook for about 30 to 45 minutes until the crust has a dark golden color.

To test for doneness, hit the bread with your knuckles and listen for a hallow sound. You may need to cook the bread longer depending on your oven since temperatures may vary.

Note:

Let the bread cool before slicing. The bread will be very crusty.

If you want a softer crust, place the cooled bread in a food safe plastic bag for a few minutes.

33 Portuguese Rolls
Papo Secos

Various regions of Portugal have their favorite bread, but the Papo Seco is the most popular bread in many homes and a staple at every restaurant serving Portuguese cuisine.

The rolls are a perfect vessel for sandwiches, dipping into soups and sauces, or served with butter. Often people will say I have a "papo seco" which literally means "dry throat" to signify they need something to drink. This recipe is adapted from a recipe given to me by Leonor Santos.

Makes approximately 2 dozen rolls

10 and ½ cups of all-purpose flour (plus more for kneading)

1 and ¼ tablespoons salt

1 and ¼ tablespoons sugar

2 packages of active dry yeast

3 tablespoons margarine (melted)

3 cups warm water

Mix water, sugar, salt and yeast in a large bowl and mix well.

Add the flour to the yeast and mix with your hand or with a dough hook. Continue mixing until a soft dough forms into a ball.

Place the dough in a greased and floured bowl. Cover, and place in a warm place until the dough has doubled in size.

When the dough has risen, shape the bread into bun shapes, make an indentation down the center with your hand and place onto a greased flat cooking pan.

Dust with flour, cover, and place on floured sheet pan. Let the rolls double in size for about 60 minutes.

Cook at 375 degrees F until golden brown for about 30 to 45 minutes.

34 Chouriço Bread
Pão de Chouriço

I make this bread very often for parties, picnics, game night or for quick snacks. My family loves it and they recognize its aroma the moment they walk in through the front door whenever I make it. I suggest you make a double batch, because this bread will disappear before you know it.

Makes 1 large or 2 small loaves

1 large chouriço or linguica (sliced to ¼ inch)

2 large onions sliced thin

1 large red pepper sliced thin

1 tablespoon olive oil

2 pounds pizza dough (or Papo Seco dough on previous page)

1 (16 oz.) package of your favorite shredded cheese (if desired)

Put your pizza dough in a large bowl and let it rise for about 30 minutes to 1 hour until doubled.

Preheat oven to 400 degrees F.

In a large skillet saute the onion and peppers in the olive oil until browned. Add the chouriço sausages and saute for about 1 minute.

Meanwhile roll out the pizza dough to desired length. You can make 1 large or 2 medium size loaves.

Spread the chouriço and onions mixture evenly over the dough. Add cheese if desired at this point. Carefully roll the dough into a long bread shape tucking in the edges of the bread underneath.

Cook for about 20 minutes or until golden brown depending on your oven. Tap the bread and listen for hollow sound. The bread will be cooked at this point.

Let cool slightly before slicing.

35 Homestyle Bread
Pão Caseiro

This recipe is adapted from my good friend Miguel Carvalho. His recipe which is from the Alentejo region of Portugal uses orange juice to give the bread a sweet taste. The first time I made this bread, I ate almost all of it myself because it was so delicious, so be warned!

Makes 2 medium loaves

7 cups flour

2 teaspoons sea salt

2 packages (2 ½ teaspoons each) active dry yeast

1 teaspoon sugar

½ cup orange juice

½ cup milk

2 and ½ cups of warm water

Dissolve the salt in the water. Put the flour in a large bowl and add the yeast, sugar, milk, orange juice and the salted water.

Mix all the ingredients with a wooden spoon until you form soft dough or you can also use your mixer with a dough hook, a bread machine on dough cycle. If dough is still extremely soft add more flour.

Cover the bowl with a warm cloth and let it rise for at least one hour or until it doubles in size. Flour your hands and place the dough on a floured surface. Knead the dough for a few minutes and separate into 2 parts.

Preheat oven to 400 degrees F.

Form the dough into round loaves and place on a lightly floured sheet pan. Let dough rest for 15 minutes.

Cook for about 30 to 40 minutes or until a dark golden crust forms. Tap bread with your knuckles to here hollow sound when it is cooked.

Cool before slicing.

36 Garlicky Rosemary Flat Bread

Broa de Alecrim

Flat bread is often called a "Bica" in my hometown. When I make this flat bread, it brings me back to memories of my family's hometown where the bread for our village was made in a communal oven built in the days of the Romans.

A male resident prepared the wood fired oven for baking the bread twice a week for the community. Early morning on those days, each family would bring their risen dough ready to bake in the oven. In payment for his services, each family would give the baker a portion of the baked bread.

Makes 1 large flat bread or 2 small

5 and ½ cups flour

1 and ¾ cups warm water

¼ cup olive oil for

1 package (2 and ½ teaspoons) yeast

1 tablespoon salt

1 tablespoon sugar

Toppings:

2 cloves garlic

¼ cup olive oil

2 or 3 teaspoons rosemary(chopped)

1 tablespoon sea salt

Make Yeast Starter First:

Place yeast, warm water, salt, and sugar in a small bowl. Stir well and let sit for about 5 minutes until bubbles form.

Place flour in a large mixing bowl. Add ¼ cup olive oil and the yeast mixture in the center and mix with dough hooks until a round ball forms. Add a few sprinkles of flour if the dough is too sticky

Remove dough from bowl and knead for about 5 minutes. Place in a floured bowl, cover with plastic and a warm towel.

Set in a warm place for 1 hour or until the dough has doubled.

Mix the other ¼ cup olive oil and garlic in a small bowl and set aside until the dough has risen.

Brush a large baking sheet with some of the olive oil.

Spread the risen dough onto the baking sheet. Use your fingers to spread the dough onto the pan and poke with fingers forming crevasses. Brush with a coating of olive oil. Set the focaccia aside in a warm place for about 1 hour until it has doubled.

Preheat oven to 425 degrees F.

When dough has risen, brush dough with the remaining olive oil and garlic, and top with the rosemary and sea salt.

side dish | acompanhamento

37 Portuguese Rice
Arroz à Portuguesa

Rice is a staple ingredient in our cuisine first brought to the Iberian Peninsula by the Arabs. During the reign of King Dom Dinis, the first written references to the cultivation of rice appeared, but during that time, rice was mainly eaten by the rich. My father was named Dinis after the king, perhaps that's why he loved rice so much! He taught me how to cook rice for the first time when I was a young school girl. He taught me that the secret to fluffy rice is to cook it using the stir fry method. Coat the rice in the hot olive oil first, and lightly stir fry it before adding the boiling water or broth. **Serves 6-8**

2 cups uncooked long grain rice

1 small onion (finely chopped)

2 tablespoons olive oil

1 chicken bouillon cube or (1 cup chicken broth, but reduce the water by 1 cup)

4 cups boiling water

1 teaspoon salt

¼ teaspoon paprika or 1 tablespoon tomato sauce (optional)

In a medium heavy casserole pan or deep skillet, saute onions on medium heat in olive oil for about 1 to 2 minutes until light golden colored.

Add the rice to the onion and olive oil mixture and let the rice stir fry for a few minutes until coated with the oil. Add the boiling water, paprika, bouillon and salt, and stir.

Let the rice come back to a boil and reduce heat to medium. Stir, cover pan and let it cook for 15 minutes.

After 15 minutes uncover the pan, stir the rice, taste, and add more salt if desired.

Turn off heat, cover and remove pan from burner until ready to serve.

How to make a rice pyramid:

Lightly grease a small ramekin or cup. Place rice in the ramekin or cup and press firmly down. Invert the rice onto your serving plate. If you notice the rice sticking to the ramekin, simply grease it again before forming each pyramid.

Note:

I like firmer rice, cook it longer if you prefer.

Never add cold water to cooking rice because the rice grains will seize up and harden.

38 Broccoli Rabe Rice
Arroz de Grelos

The basic rice recipe in the previous page is simple to prepare. To make variations on the rice, simply add vegetables such as broccoli rabe, broccoli, cauliflower, or even peas and carrots a few minutes before the end of the rice's cooking process. **Serves 6-8**

1 small bunch broccoli rabe (washed and chopped)

2 cups of long grain rice

3 tablespoons of olive oil

1 small onion (fined minced)

2 garlic cloves (finely minced)

1 bay leaf

4 cups of boiling water

1 teaspoon salt

Parboil the broccoli rabe in boiling water for about 5 minutes to reduce bitterness. Drain.

In a heavy saucepan, saute the onion, garlic and bay leaf in the olive oil for a few minutes until the onion is translucent.

Add the water, and salt and let come to a boil.

Add the rice and broccoli rabe. Let come to a boil, cover and cook for 15 minutes on medium heat stirring once in a while.

Remove from heat, stir, taste for doneness and let the rice sit covered for a few minutes to absorb excess moisture.

Fluff gently with a fork before serving.

39 Portuguese Style Green Bean Rice
Arroz de Feijão Verde

You can use any varieties of green beans in this recipe. The rice pairs well with meats, poultry or fish. **Serves 6-8**

2 cups fresh or frozen green beans

2 cups long grain rice

½ small onion (finely chopped)

1 small very ripe tomato (seeded)

2 tablespoons of olive oil

2 cups of chicken or vegetable stock

2 cups boiling water

1 teaspoon salt

Saute the onion on medium heat with the olive oil in a medium size heavy saucepan until translucent.

Add the tomato, cook for about 1 minute and crush with your spoon or a fork.

Add the water and stock and cook until boiling.

Add the rice and salt. Cover and cook for 10 minutes on medium heat.

Uncover the rice, and add the green beans. Stir, cover, and let cook for another 10 minutes on medium heat. Stir once in a while.

If you notice the rice needs liquid add only ½ cup of boiling water or broth at a time until the rice is cooked to your desired preference.

40 Chick Pea Rice
Arroz com Grão

Chick peas add a nutty crunch to this rice. It will pair well with fish or meats. **Serves 6-8**

2 cups rice

4 cups boiling water

1 small onion (chopped)

2 tablespoon olive oil

1 tablespoon any tomato sauce

1 teaspoon salt

1 small can chick peas (drained and rinsed)

1 teaspoon parsley (finely chopped) (optional)

In a medium heavy sauce pan, on medium heat saute onion in olive oil until translucent.

Add the rice and stir to coat with the olive oil. Let the rice stir fry for about 2 minutes on medium heat.

Add the water, tomato sauce and salt, and let come to a boil. Reduce the heat to medium, stir, and cover.

Let the rice cook on medium for 15 to 20 minutes stirring a few times.

After the rice has cooked add the drained chick peas, stir, cover pan, and let the rice sit until ready to serve.

41 Tomato Flavored Rice
Arroz de Tomate

This rice recipe is the most popular. It's a perfect match for fried fish fillets but it also can be served with your grilled meats or roasts. **Serves 6-8**

1 small onion (finely minced)

1 garlic clove (minced)

2 tablespoons olive oil

1 bay leaf

1 cup very ripe crushed tomatoes

2 cups rice

3 cups boiling water

1 cup of chicken broth

Parsley for garnish

In a heavy saucepan saute the onion, garlic and bay leaf in the olive oil for about 2 minutes on medium heat.

Add the tomato, and cook until it reduces down a little and thickens.

Crush the tomato with a potato masher or a fork. If you like the tomatoes chunky just leave them as is.

Add the rice, salt, pinch of sugar, broth and boiling water. Stir the rice, cover and cook for about 15 to 20 minutes on medium heat stirring a few times.

Remove from heat and set aside until ready to serve.

Note:

Add more tomatoes if you want a more tomato flavored rice.

42 Portuguese Style Roast Potatoes
Batatas Assadas

The secret to perfect roasted potatoes is to rub them with good olive oil, then add salt and butter. I also add onions which give the potatoes a sweet and savory taste. Then let them cook at 400 degrees tossing the pan gently every 15 minutes. Use a spatula to turn them over. Let them cook longer to obtain a really crispy skin. **Serves 8-10**

2 pounds potatoes (cut into quarters or desired lengths)

1 small onion (chopped)

1 teaspoon salt

1 teaspoon garlic powder

½ teaspoon pepper

1 teaspoon paprika

¼ stick of melted margarine or butter

¼ cup olive oil

Place all ingredients into a large mixing bowl. Toss well to coat potatoes.

Place seasoned potatoes into a medium size greased baking pan and shake pan to spread evenly.

Cook at 400 F for about 1 hour or until fork tender.

Note:

Toss potatoes every 15 minutes to achieve a crispy texture.

Use a spatula to turn the potatoes over. Do not use a fork.

43 Garlicky Roasted Punched Potatoes

Batatas a Murro

These garlicky potatoes are a delicious side dish and so easy to make that you may never peel another potato again. Just wash and pat them dry, coat them with olive oil and salt, and then bake. I make the garlic oil by placing the oil in a small pan or microwave dish, cook for a minute or two and then drizzle the oil over the cooked potatoes. These potatoes are often served with baked bacalhau or fish, but pair wonderfully with any meat.

Serves 6-8

2 pounds small potatoes (unpeeled)

Coarse salt

4 to 6 cloves garlic (finely chopped)

½ to 1 cup of olive oil

Wash and scrub the potatoes. Remove any blemishes and pat dry. Pierce with a fork in a couple of spots.

Coat drizzle of olive oil and rub with salt. Place potatoes in small oven proof dish or pan. I use an oven to table dish for easy serving.

Cook at 400 F for 45 minutes to 1 hour depending on your oven.

Meanwhile, make garlic oil:

In a small saucepan or in the microwave, heat the oil and add the garlic. Cook on low for a minute or two until the garlic turn slightly golden. Do not overcook or the garlic will become bitter!

To test potatoes for doneness, pierce them with a fork or gently squeeze a potato holding your oven mitt. The potato should be soft.

When the potatoes are ready, punch them down with your fist wrapped in a clean dish towel or with a meat mallet until they "pop" open.

Note:

The potatoes are hot, be careful!

When ready to serve gently spread open the potatoes and pour the warm garlic oil over them.

44 Potato Omelet with Presunto
Omelete de Batata e Presunto

When I was still living at home with my parents, I was often awakened at 6 six o'clock in the morning with the aroma created by the presunto or the chouriço grilling from the omelets my mother made for my father's lunch.

When her grandchildren came along, she added very fine sliced potato fries to the omelets. These omelets became the grandchildren's favorite lunch at Avo's (Grandmother's) house

Serves 2-3

6 whole eggs

2 cups of cooked thin sliced French fries or potato chips

2 slices Presunto or ½ small sliced chouriço

¼ cup onion (finely chopped)

2 teaspoons fresh parsley (chopped)

Olive oil

Crushed black pepper

Cheese (optional)

In a large bowl, beat eggs until foamy and add the chips or potatoes. Let sit for about 5 minutes to soften.

Meanwhile, on high heat brown the onions and presunto or chouriço in 3 tablespoons of olive oil until crispy.

Add the egg and potato mixture to the pan. Add 1 teaspoon of the parsley.

Cook on medium for 3 to 5 minutes shaking the pan so it doesn't stick.

Cover the pan with a large dish, flip the omelet back in the skillet uncooked side down and cook for another 2 minutes.

Top with cheese and parsley if desired.

45 Portuguese Style Potato Salad
Salada Russa

My Godmother taught me this recipe when I was very young. The first time I tried it, I didn't like it because it had peas, carrots, green beans, and something called "mayonnaise" which I never heard before in my life. She called it "Russian Salad", another word I'd never heard before. Today, this has become my family's favorite potato salad during the summer months. **Serves 6-12**

---

2 ½ pounds potatoes (chopped into 1 inch cubes)

½ of a small onion (finely chopped)

1 cup fresh or frozen petite peas

1 cup fresh or frozen carrots chopped to ¼ inch cubes

1 cup fresh or frozen cut green beans (optional)

1 tablespoon minced parsley

2 teaspoons salt

½ teaspoon pepper

½ teaspoon garlic powder

2 tablespoons Italian salad dressing or 1 tablespoon each of olive oil and vinegar

½ cup mayonnaise

6 hardboiled eggs (optional)

Place the potatoes into salted water and let come to a boil. After 5 minutes, add the carrots, and green beans.

Let the vegetables come to another boil and cook for about 5 minutes longer.

Pierce the potatoes to be sure they're cooked. Add peas and onions during the last 5 minutes of cooking time.

Drain the potatoes in a colander and let cool. When cool, place in a large bowl.

Toss in all of the remaining ingredients except the eggs. Fold with plastic spatula, stirring gently not to break the potatoes apart.

Chop eggs into fourths and add to potatoes. Place the salad into serving dish and garnish with parsley and a sprinkle of paprika.

Note:

Store up to 3 days in the refrigerator.

46 Tomato, Egg and Potato Salad
Salada de Tomate e Batatas com Ovos

This salad is simply easy to make in one salad bowl and a perfect go to dish on your busy days. During the summer months, I make this salad at least once a week with Portuguese heirloom tomatoes that I grow in our garden. It pairs well with all grilled meats and fish and can be served as a main dish salad. **Serves 4-6**

---

6 ripe tomatoes (sliced thick or quartered)

6 boiled new potatoes (chopped into 2 inch cubes)

6 hardboiled eggs (cut into quarters)

1 small onion (sliced)

Olives (optional)

Dressing:

¼ cup white wine vinegar

¼ cup olive oil

Salt

Pepper

2 tablespoons parsley (chopped)

Basil (chopped)

Arrange the potatoes, tomatoes and eggs in a large serving platter.

Place dressing ingredients in a jar with a lid or in a bowl and mix well.

Top salad with dressing, toss gently and serve.

main dish | prato principal

47 Portuguese Shellfish Stew
Mariscada

This is my family's favorite seafood dish which I learned from a Portuguese chef many years ago. The combination of ingredients and spices blend perfectly with the fresh seafood and creates a rich flavorful broth. The seafood will pair perfectly with Portuguese rice.

Serves 2-4

1 fresh whole uncooked lobster (chopped into quarters)

1 pound raw, peeled and de-veined Shrimp

1 pound mussels or little neck clams (washed)

½ pound scallops

½ pound of squid (cut into rings)

1 small onion (finely chopped)

2 cloves garlic (minced)

¼ cup olive oil

1 cup Vinho Verde or white wine

1 teaspoon salt

1 teaspoon paprika

1 cup chicken broth

2 tablespoons butter

2 tablespoons chopped cilantro (garnish)

Squeeze of lemon juice

Dash of hot sauce (if desired)

Preparation:

Saute the onions and garlic in the olive oil in a large heavy skillet on medium heat for one minute. Add lobster, and saute for a few minutes on low heat. Add clams, wine, paprika, salt, bouillon cube and pepper, cover and let cook for 5 minutes.

Add the chicken broth, shrimp, and scallops, cover and cook on medium heat for another 5 minutes or until the clams open.

Add butter and continue cooking for another 5 minutes for the butter to thicken the sauce. Taste for saltiness and add hot sauce or more seasonings if desired.

Add the chopped cilantro and top with a squeeze of lemon juice before serving.

Serve with rice.

48 Baked Stuffed Shrimp Portuguese Style
Camarão Recheado

This baked stuffed shrimp recipe which I learned from a Portuguese chef many years ago has been passed down through the years in my family. Portuguese rolls are the base in the stuffing which gives great texture and taste. It's perfect for stuffing fish, chicken, or even vegetables such as mushrooms or zucchini.

You'll never throw away old papo secos again once you make this recipe. Simply place old rolls in freezer bags for making this at a later date. The stuffing freezes very well, so I suggest you make a double batch and then freeze one half in freezer bags for the next time you make it. **Serves 4-6**

2 pounds extra-large shrimp (about 10 to 12 per pound) (peeled & deveined with tails on)

3 papo seco rolls (preferably day old)

15 Ritz crackers or any brand of buttery crackers

1 package garlic flavored croutons

½ cup celery (finely minced)

½ cup onion (finely minced)

3 tablespoons olive oil

½ stick (4 tablespoons) of melted butter

1 pound of small or medium raw shrimp (peeled & deveined)

¼ cup white wine

1 teaspoon paprika

½ teaspoon garlic powder

½ teaspoon salt

1 small chicken bouillon cube

2 tablespoons parsley (finely chopped)

Prepare Shrimp:

Peel both the small and large shrimp and place into separate bowls. Reserve the shells.

Cook the shells in 3 cups of water and a pinch of salt for about 8 minutes. Strain the broth into a big bowl and let it cool. Throw away the shells.

In a small skillet, saute the onion and celery with olive oil for 5 minutes until translucent on medium low heat.

Remove the onions and celery with a slotted spoon and leave a little of the olive oil in the pan. Let the onion mix cool in a small bowl.

In the same skillet with the leftover olive oil, add the small shrimp, bouillon cube, garlic, salt and paprika.

Cook for 1 minute until the shrimp turns slightly pink. Add the wine and cook for another 3 minutes until the wine reduces.

Remove the skillet from the heat and let the shrimp mixture cool while you prepare the bread stuffing.

Prepare the stuffing:

Chop the bread into small chunks and place into the bowl with the shrimp broth

Mash the bread with your fingers or a fork until no lumps remain. The bread should be the constancy of wet dough like batter. If you find the bread too dry add a little more broth or water. Let the bread absorb the liquid.

Crumble the crackers with your hands and add to the bread. Add the cooled onions and celery. The stuffing will be wet, but if you find it too runny add more bread or crackers.

Add the shrimp and parsley into the stuffing and mix well. Taste and add more salt if desired.

Set aside while you prepare the shrimp for stuffing.

Prepare and Assemble Shrimp:

Prepare the large shrimp by gently deveining and slicing at the curved end in the butterfly cut.

Grease a cooking tray with butter or margarine and place each shrimp butterfly up in the pan. Place 1 tablespoon or more of the stuffing into the center of each shrimp.

Place the croutons in a ziploc plastic bag. Close tightly making sure no air is left inside. Crumble the croutons into very fine crumbs. This should yield about 1 and ½ cups.

Sprinkle 1 teaspoon or more of the crumbled croutons over each shrimp. Don't be afraid to use all of the crumb mix.

Curve the tails gently over the stuffing to form a "c" shape. Add one teaspoon of melted butter over the top of each shrimp.

Cook in a 375 degree F oven for about 15 to 20 minutes until the shrimp turn pink and golden brown. Remove shrimp from the oven promptly so they don't dry out.

Drizzle more melted butter on top before serving.

Note:

You can leave the shrimp in the oven on very low heat to keep them warm before serving. Be careful since they may become dry if the heat is too high.

Never throw away old papo secos, simply place them in freezer bags for making this stuffing at a later date.

Make a double batch of the stuffing and freeze it by placing in freezer safe plastic bags or bowls.

49 Shrimp with Rice and Sweet Peas
Arroz de Camarão

This recipe is good enough to serve your guests on a special occasion but you can also make it when you want a quick and easy recipe on your meatless days. Sweet paprika and white wine adds a savory flavor to the shrimp creating a perfect combination with the fluffy rice. **Serves 6-8**

---

1 small onion (finely chopped)

3 tablespoons olive oil

2 cups long grain rice

3 cups boiling water

1 cup chicken broth

1 teaspoon salt

1 cup frozen sweet peas

1 to 2 pounds medium raw peeled deveined shrimp

1 teaspoon paprika

1 teaspoon white wine

In a heavy medium pan, saute ½ of the onion in 2 tablespoons of the olive oil until translucent on medium high heat.

Add the rice and stir fry it for about 1 minute to coat with the olive oil. Slowly add the boiling water, salt and chicken broth and stir. When the rice comes to a boil, cover and reduce heat to medium.

Cook for 15 to 20 minutes stirring only once or twice. Cover, and remove from heat.

Shrimp and Peas preparation:

In a small skillet on high, saute the remaining onion in 1 tablespoon of olive oil until translucent. Add the shrimp and cook for about 1 minute or until the shrimp turns pink.

Add the paprika and wine, and let cook for 1 minute longer. Add the peas, stir, and cook for 1 minute.

Stir the shrimp and peas into the rice and serve.

50 Seafood Rice
Arroz de Marisco

The combination of seafood and rice cooked with flavorful spices and then baked in the oven develops a crunchy top layer with a nutty texture. This classic dish is often served at weddings and special celebrations. **Serves 4-8**

1 whole fresh lobster (cut into pieces)

1 pound uncooked medium shrimp (peeled and deveined)

½ pound scallops

1 pound little neck clams (washed)

1 pound mussels (washed and cleaned)

2 cups long grain uncooked rice

1 small onion (finely chopped)

1 clove garlic (finely chopped)

1 cup ripe tomatoes (crushed)

½ of a small red bell pepper (chopped)

1 cup of uncooked peas

Pinch of saffron

1 teaspoon salt

4 cups chicken broth

1 teaspoon paprika

½ cup Vinho Verde or white wine

Cilantro for garnish (optional)

Preparation:

Preheat oven to 350 degrees F. Saute the onion, red peppers and garlic in the olive oil, in a large deep oven proof pan or casserole dish. Add the lobster pieces and brown for a few minutes.

Add the wine, tomatoes, paprika, and salt, and cook for about 5 minutes until reduced. Add the broth and bring to a boil.

Add the rice and saffron and stir while cooking for about 5 minutes on high heat. Taste and add more seasoning if needed.

Remove the pan from the burner. Stir in the peas. Arrange the shrimp, scallops, clams, and mussels, evenly submerged on top of the rice.

Bake in the oven uncovered for about 30 minutes until the rice and seafood is fully cooked and the clams open.

51 Clams with Chouriço
Ameijoas com Chouriço

This surf and turf combination of the spicy chouriço and juicy clams creates a tangy sauce. Serve with crusty bread for dipping into the broth. **Serves 2**

2 pounds little neck or manila clams (washed and scrubbed)

1 chouriço sausage (sliced into ¼ inch slices)

½ small onion (finely chopped)

2 cloves garlic cloves (chopped)

1 small very ripe tomato (crushed)

2 tablespoons olive oil

½ cup white wine

½ teaspoon piri piri or hot sauce (optional)

2 tablespoons cilantro (finely chopped)

Squeeze of lemon juice

Saute the onions and garlic and olive oil in a medium skillet until translucent.

Add the chouriço and saute for about 2 minutes.

Add the tomatoes, wine, hot sauce and clams. Mix, cover and cook for about 5 to 8 minutes on medium heat until the clams open.

Top with a squeeze of lemon juice.

Add the cilantro and as a garnish before serving.

52 Codfish à Gomes de Sa Style
Bacalhau à Gomes de Sa

This dish originates from the city of Porto, Portugal and is named for its creator Gomes de Sa. This classic is one of the most popular recipes using bacalhau and is featured on most Portuguese restaurant menus.

I learned this recipe many years ago from a great Portuguese chef. It's the most requested dish by my friends and family. This classic is most often served during the Consoada dinner on Christmas Eve, and at many celebrations.

Serves 6-10

2 pounds boneless salt cod

4 pounds small potatoes
(peeled and cut into 1 inch slices)

2 large onions

3 gloves chopped garlic

1 bay leaf

1 teaspoon salt

1 teaspoon pepper

1 cup olive oil

6 hardboiled eggs

1 cup olives

2 teaspoons chopped parsley

2 cloves of chopped garlic or 1 teaspoon garlic powder

½ teaspoon salt for onions

How to rehydrate salt cod:

If you have a whole salt cod, cut it into portions of 4 x 6 inches. Rinse with cold water and place covered in large pan with cold water for 2 days in the refrigerator, changing the water twice a day until the heavy saltiness is gone.

If your cod is very thick you may need to soak it longer.

To test for saltiness, cut a small piece of the cod and taste. It should taste like cod but still have some saltiness.

Do not let the cod sit for more than 3 days in the water since it will become mealy and tasteless.

Freeze in serving portions in plastic bags.

Prepare Cod and Potatoes:

Place potatoes covered with cold water in large pan. Add salt, bring to a boil and cook for 10 minutes.

Place codfish over boiling potatoes and cook for about 8 minutes or until flaky.

Remove cod fish from pan and set aside to cool.

When cooled, remove any bones and flake the cod into strips.

Potatoes should be cooked but pierce with fork to check for done ness. Drain potatoes and set aside to cool.

Slice the potatoes into ¼ inch slices and set aside.

Prepare Onions:

In large skillet, saute sliced onions, garlic, ½ tsp salt and bay leaf with ½ cup of the olive oil until golden brown.

Remove the bay leaf and let the onions cool for a few minutes.

Assemble:

Grease a large deep oven proof pan with olive oil. Start layering the potatoes first, then the flaked cod and finally the onions.

Drizzle olive oil and pepper over each layer ending with an onion layer on top.
Add garlic powder to each layer if you love garlic.

Cover with foil and cook at 350 degrees F for about 20 minutes. Cook uncovered for another 5 to 10 minutes to desired crispness.

Remove pan from oven.

Slice eggs and place them on top of onion layer. Add more salt, pepper or garlic if desired.

Return the casserole back into the oven on warm heat until ready to serve.

Add parsley more olive oil and olives as garnish before serving.

101

53 Codfish with Chick Peas
Bacalhau com Grão

Codfish with chick peas is an authentic old recipe that is one of the most popular ways to eat bacalhau and has been served for centuries. Black eyed peas are often substituted for the chick peas in the recipe. **Serves 2**

1 pound boneless salt cod
(cut into 2, 8 ounce portions)

2 cups water

1 sliced onion

2 cups cooked chick peas

Vinaigrette:

¼ cup olive oil

¼ cup white wine vinegar

1 clove of garlic (finely minced)

¼ teaspoon salt

¼ teaspoon black pepper

Garnish:

2 tablespoons parsley (chopped)

1 tablespoon onion (finely minced)

Make the vinaigrette in a medium bowl by mixing the ingredients together and set aside.

Meanwhile, poach the codfish in a medium pan filled with about 2 cups of water and the slice of onion. Cook at slow rolling bowl for about 8 to 10 minutes on medium heat.

Remove the codfish from the pan, drain, and cover to keep warm.

Heat the chick peas on low heat. Drain, and place with the cod on a serving dish.

Pour the vinaigrette on top and serve.

Add more olive oil and seasonings if desired.

Add Garnish.

54 Codfish à Braz Style
Bacalhau à Braz

This recipe is named after its creator, and originated hundreds of years ago in the Estremadura (meaning extremities), on the coastline region of central Portugal. This seacoast is known for bountiful fishing waters, and its consistent wind that creates record breaking ocean waves. **Serves 2**

½ pound boneless salt cod (finely shredded)

2 potatoes (peeled and cut into small match stick size)

3 eggs

¼ cup thinly sliced onion

1 clove garlic

1 bay leaf

1 tablespoon parsley (chopped)

Olives for garnish

Salt and pepper to taste

2 tablespoons olive oil

Oil for frying potatoes

Fry the potatoes in very hot oil and set aside.

Saute onions, garlic and bay leaf until translucent in olive oil.

Stir the cod fish into the onions and cook for about 1 minute.

Remove bay leaf. Add eggs and cook on very low heat until lightly cooked.

Gently stir the potato sticks and parsley into to the eggs.

Add salt and pepper to taste.

Garnish with olives and parsley.

55 Baked Codfish with Potatoes and Onions
Bacalhau Assado

Codfish with potatoes and olive oil are a match made in heaven. This dish is one the most popular recipes for bacalhau and traditionally served for Christmas Eve dinner. This is my sister Isabel's recipe.

Serves 4-6

4 (6 to 8 oz.) portions of salt cod with bone	Preheat oven to 400 degrees F.
12 to 20 small round potatoes	Wash and dry the potatoes, slice them into quarters, and par boil for about 10 minutes. Drain and set aside.
2 large onions (sliced)	
1 large bell pepper	Coat the bottom of a large baking pan with a few tablespoons of olive oil.
½ to 1 cup olive oil	
1 bay leaf	Place the cod in the pan and surround with the potatoes.
4 cloves garlic (chopped)	Cover the cod with the sliced onions, pepper, garlic and bay leaf and coat with the remaining olive oil.
Black pepper	
2 teaspoons chopped parsley	Cook for 35 minutes.
Black olives for garnish	Pierce potatoes for doneness. If they are not fully cooked remove the cod from the pan and continue to cook the potatoes longer.
	When ready to serve, garnish with black olives, olive oil from the baking pan, and parsley.

56 Codfish à Zé do Pipo Style
Bacalhau à Zé do Pipo

This dish originates from the city of Porto, and is named after its creator, Zé do Pipo, who owned a famous restaurant in that city during the 1960's. The chef won a national cooking contest with this recipe and since then, many restaurants have adopted it into their menus.
Serves 4-6

1 pound salt cod (cut into 4 portions)	Cook potatoes in boiling water for about 25 minutes. Remove from heat, drain, and add the milk, butter, egg yolk and pepper. Mash and set aside.
8 large potatoes (peeled cut into quarters)	
1 teaspoon salt	Coat the cod in flour and fry in the olive oil on medium low heat until golden. Place on paper towels to soak off excess oil.
½ cup olive oil	
1 large sliced onion	Saute the onions, garlic and bay leaf in the same olive oil that you cooked the fish in, until lightly browned. Remove the bay leaf.
1 diced garlic clove	
1 bay leaf	Place the cod portions in a large oven safe casserole dish or in individual serving size dishes.
¼ cup flour for frying codfish	
2 tablespoons butter	Cover the cod with the onion mixture and surround with the mashed potatoes. Coat each piece with a few tablespoons of mayonnaise followed by a slice of red pepper.
1 cup milk	
1 egg yolk	
½ cup mayonnaise	Bake at 350 degrees F for 20 minutes until the mayonnaise turns golden brown.
1 small roasted red pepper	
Black olives	Garnish with olives and parsley.
Parsley	

57 Spanish Style Codfish Casserole
Bacalhau com Molho à Espanhola

My mother learned this recipe from the Spanish peddlers that often spent the night at her bed and breakfast. She also learned how to speak Spanish from them which amazed me. You can substitute the cod with any flaky fish in this recipe, but only add the fish to the rice during the last 5 minutes of cooking. **Serves 4-6**

1 pound boneless salt cod

2 cups long grain rice

1 teaspoon salt

2 tablespoons of olive oil

1 small onion diced

1small red pepper (sliced thin)

1 bay leaf

1 small green pepper (sliced thin)

2 small crushed ripe tomatoes

2 cloves garlic (chopped)

2 teaspoons parsley (chopped)

Salt and pepper

Black olives

Cook the cod fish in 4 cups boiling water for 8 to 10 minutes. Drain, saving the water, and flake cod into strips and set aside.

Saute the onions, garlic, pepper, and bay leaf in the olive oil for about 3 minutes in a medium heavy skillet until translucent.

Add the tomatoes and cod fish, and cook at medium for 5 to 8 minutes. Set aside until the rice is ready.

Rice Preparation:

Place the 4 cups of water in a large pan and bring to a boil. Add 1 teaspoon of salt and the rice. Reduce the heat to medium, cover and cook for 15 minutes.

Add the codfish to the rice and stir to incorporate. Cook on low heat for about 5 minutes until the flavors have incorporated.

Garnish with parsley and olives before serving.

58 Pan Fried Fish Fillets
Filetes

Portugal is a seafaring nation with a well-developed fishing industry. It has Europe's highest fish consumption per capita and is among the top four in the world. This recipe creates a light battered fried fish with a lemon flavor that pairs perfectly with Portuguese rice. **Serves 4-6**

2 pounds fish fillets (preferably cod or haddock but you can use any flaky white fish) (cut into portions ½ inches thick)

2 eggs

1 tablespoon water

Flour

Salt and pepper

½ teaspoon garlic powder (optional)

1 lemon

1 and ½ cups oil for frying (preferably corn or vegetable)

1 tablespoon olive oil

Lemon slices

½ lemon

Season the fish with the salt, pepper and garlic. Squeeze the juice from half of the lemon over the fish and set aside for about 5 minutes. (Do not let the fish sit in the lemon for more than a few minutes or the acidity will dissolve it.)

Beat the eggs with the water in a medium bowl.

Place the flour in a medium bowl. Using one dry and one wet hand method, coat the fish with the egg, shaking off excess egg then dredge with flour.

Place oil in a heavy frying pan to reach ½ inches deep. Heat to medium. Test the oil by placing one tip of the fish fillet into the oil. It will sizzle when ready.

Cook 4 to 6 pieces of fish in batches, in the hot oil for about 4 minutes on each side until golden brown. Adjust the heat if the fish gets browned too quickly.

Place the fillets on paper towels to absorb any grease. Garnish with lemon wedges before serving.

59 Stewed Squid
Lulas Guisadas

The squid in this recipe cooks in a tomato and wine broth making it tender and juicy. This recipe was first taught to me by my dear mother in law many years ago when I was first married because it was one of my husband's favorite dishes. **Serves 4-6**

2 pounds of cleaned squid

1 small chouriço (sliced)

¼ cup olive oil

1 large onion (sliced)

1 large red bell pepper

2 bay leaves

4 cloves garlic (chopped

1 cup very ripe tomatoes (crushed)

1cup white wine

Squeeze of lemon

2 tablespoons parsley (chopped)

Slice the squid into rings about 1 inch in thick, and cut the tentacles into chunks.

Saute the onion, garlic, pepper and bay leaf in the olive oil. Add the tomatoes, wine, salt and pepper and cook for a few minutes.

Add the squid and chourico and cook on low medium heat for about 20 to 30 minutes stirring often until the squid becomes tender. Add water if you find the sauce becoming too thick.

Serve with boiled potatoes.

Garnish with a squeeze of lemon and parsley before serving.

60 Garlicky Grilled Squid
Lulas Grelhadas

These grilled squid are garlicky, sweet, and tender. They cook in only a few minutes on each side so don't overcook them. **Serves 4-6**

---

2 pounds cleaned raw squid (cut into 2 inch strips lengthwise)

1 teaspoon salt

Pepper

Olive oil

Vinaigrette:

½ cup olive oil

½ cup white wine vinegar

5 cloves garlic (finely minced)

2 tablespoons
 onion (finely minced)

Salt

Pepper

2 tablespoons parsley (finely minced)

Season the squid and tentacles with the salt and pepper and coat with olive oil.

Grill on very hot charcoal or gas grill for about 4 minutes on each size until golden and set aside on a warm dish.

Meanwhile, prepare the vinaigrette in a small bowl by mixing all the ingredients very well to incorporate.

Pour vinaigrette over cooked squid. Garnish with parsley.

Serve with boiled, punched roast potatoes, or rice.

61 Portuguese Seafood Stew
Caldeirada de Peixe

Portugal's coast is bountiful with seafood harvested by its famous fishermen. Fish and seafood are the main ingredient in many of the nation's dishes. This one pot chowder is said to have originated from these fisherman while on their expeditions in the Atlantic Ocean. It incorporates the flavors from the seafood and the spices brought back from the explorations around the world. **Serves 4-6**

1 pound of potatoes (cut into cubes)

2 tablespoons olive oil

3 medium onions (thinly sliced)

1 red bell pepper (chopped)

3 garlic cloves (minced)

2 bay leaves

3 very ripe tomatoes (crushed)

1 cup Vinho Verde or white wine

1 cup fish or chicken broth

2 to 3 cups water

½ pound shrimp (peeled and deveined)

½ pound little neck clams (washed)

½ pound fresh bone in fish (cut into 2 inch pieces)

½ pound boneless flaky white fish (cut into 2 inch pieces)

½ pound squid (cleaned and cut into 1 inch rings)

2 teaspoons salt

½ teaspoon paprika

Cilantro for garnish

Preparation:

In a large casserole pan, saute the onion, garlic, bay leaf and peppers in olive oil until translucent for about 5 minutes. Add the tomatoes, paprika and wine and cook for about 5 minutes until the wine reduces down. Add the potatoes, bouillon and water and cook for about 15 minutes on high heat. Add the seafood, by layering, fish with bone first, then the squid, clams, and the flaky white fish last.

Cover and cook on medium for about 10 to 15 minutes on low medium heat until the clams open. Taste and add more seasoning if desired. Top with chopped cilantro before serving.

62 Octopus Rice
Arroz de Polvo

My mother was a frugal cook and very creative in the kitchen when it came to leftovers. This is her recipe and one of my favorite rice dishes using leftover octopus from our family's Christmas Eve dinner. **Serves 6-8**

1 pound cooked octopus (cut into chunks)

1 small onion (minced)

1 garlic clove (minced)

2 tablespoons olive oil

1 small very ripe tomato (crushed)

2 cups uncooked long grain rice

4 cups hot chicken broth

½ teaspoon salt

Parsley for garnish

In a heavy skillet saute the onion and garlic in the olive oil on medium heat until translucent.

Add the Octopus and tomato and cook for a few minutes to incorporate the flavors.

Add the rice, and the hot broth, and let it come to rolling boil on high heat. Reduce heat to medium, stir, cover and cook for about 15 minutes.

If you find the rice has become dry and needs to cook longer, add more broth or a little boiling water.

Add more seasoning if needed, garnish with parsley and serve.

63 Baked Octopus with Potatoes
Polvo Assado com Batatas

Octopus is harvested off the coastal waters of Portugal and considered a delicacy. Some chefs beat the tentacles with a mallet, and some suggest adding a wine cork to the cooking liquid to tenderize it. I cook it with an onion for 1 to 1and ½ hours but some may require a longer time. This recipe is often served on Christmas Eve but also enjoyed all year long.

Serves 4-6

2 pounds of octopus	Cook the octopus whole by boiling it with the salt and onion in enough water to cover it with 2 extra inches of water. Cook for 1 hour or longer until the octopus is tender.
1 large onion	
1 large onion (chopped)	
2 pounds of small round potatoes (washed and dry)	Place the potatoes in a deep baking dish and season with salt and pepper. Top with ½ of the raw chopped onion and ½ cup olive oil and cook at 400 F for about 30 minutes shaking the pan once in a while.
1 large red bell pepper (chopped)	
3 cloves garlic (chopped)	Saute remaining onion, red pepper, garlic, and bay leaf in ¼ cup olive oil for about 5 minutes. Add the vinegar and cook for a minute. Set aside.
½ cup of olive oil	
¼ cup of olive oil	
1 tablespoon white vinegar	When octopus is cooked, drain and place in the pan with the potatoes.
1 teaspoon salt	Pour the onion mixture over the potatoes and octopus.
1 teaspoon pepper	
1 bay leaf	Cook at 350 degrees F until the potatoes are fully cooked.
Parsley for garnish	Garnish with chopped parsley before serving.

64 Braised Rabbit with Rice
Arroz de Coelho

Rabbit has more protein than beef and has less cholesterol and calories than any other meat. You can find fresh rabbit in many butcher shops and specialty markets.

Serves 4-8

1 (2 to 3) pound fresh rabbit (cut into small pieces)

2 cups long grain rice

2 teaspoons of salt

Pepper

¼ cup olive oil

1 small onion (minced)

1 small tomato (crushed)

1 garlic clove (minced)

1 bay leaf

1 fresh rosemary sprig

½ cup red wine

4 cups boiling water

Parsley for garnish

Marinate the rabbit in salt, pepper, rosemary, and the white wine and set aside for at least 1 hour in the refrigerator or overnight.

In a large heavy pan, saute the onions, garlic and bay leaf in the olive oil until translucent.

Drain the rabbit, remove the rosemary, reserve the marinade, and place the meat in the pan with the onion. Cook on medium heat and brown the rabbit on each side.

Add the reserved marinade, 1 cup of water, and the tomato. Cook for 45 minutes on low medium heat stirring frequently.

Add the rice and stir to absorb the flavors. Add the boiling water to the pan, stir and cover.

Cook on medium heat for 20 minutes stirring frequently until cooked. You may need to add more boiling water if the rice needs to cook longer.

Uncover, stir and add seasoning if needed.

Garnish with parsley and serve.

65 Rabbit Stew Hunter Style
Coelho à Caçador

This rabbit stew is a classic recipe made on special occasions. It's simple to make because it cooks in one pan. **Serves 4-6**

---

2 to 3 pounds bone in rabbit meat (cut into pieces)

1 large onion (chopped)

2 large very ripe tomatoes

2 garlic cloves (chopped)

1 cup of red wine

1 or 2 cups water

2 bay leaves

1 teaspoon salt

1 teaspoon pepper

1 tablespoon olive oil

Marinate the rabbit with all ingredients except the tomatoes in a large bowl. Place in the refrigerator overnight.

Take the rabbit out of the refrigerator 30 minutes before cooking.

Heat the oil in a very large oven proof pan. Drain the rabbit reserving the marinade.

Cook the rabbit in the skillet on medium heat until it browns on both sides.

Add the onions, leftover marinade and tomatoes and cook for 20 minutes on medium heat. Add a little water to thin sauce if needed.

Add 1 or 2 cups of water and continue cooking. Add more water if the sauce dries out.

Heat the oven to 350 degrees F.

Place the skillet in the oven and cook the rabbit for about 1 hour until the meat is falling off the bone.

Serve with rice or boiled potatoes.

66 Roast Paprika Chicken
Frango Assado

Sunday dinners in a Portuguese home usually include a roasted chicken and every home cook has their own technique for this dish. This recipe is simple to prepare and comes out perfect every time. You can be creative and add your own spices to make it your own. Serve with my roasted potatoes or rice recipe. **Serves 4-6**

1 large roasting chicken	Mix the seasonings together in a small bowl.
2 teaspoon salt	Wash the chicken and pat dry. Rub the chicken with olive oil and margarine, then coat with the seasonings.
1 teaspoon pepper	
2 teaspoons garlic powder	Insert onion, celery and parsley into cavity. Pour the wine into the cavity. Squeeze the lemon juice over the chicken and then place the rind into the cavity.
2 teaspoons paprika	
1 small onion (quartered)	
1 small celery stalk (chopped)	Leave chicken marinating for at least 2 hours in the refrigerator, overnight.
½ of a lemon	When ready to cook, place the marinated room temperature chicken in a large roasting pan. Cook at 400 degrees F for 1 and ½ hours for a small 3 to 4 pound chicken.
2 tablespoons olive oil	
1 tablespoon butter or margarine	
1 sprig fresh parsley	**Note:**
½ cup white wine	Even though your timer on the chicken may pop up, let the chicken cook longer until it's crispy and golden colored.

67 Rosemary Chicken with Lemon and Paprika
Frango Assado com Alecrim

I make a roasted chicken at least once a week and it never disappoints. I've incorporated paprika into this chicken rosemary dish which adds sweetness and pairs well with the zesty lemon.

Cook the sweet potatoes cook along with the chicken in the same pan.

Serves 4-6

1 roaster chicken (3 to 4 pounds)

1 Lemon

2 teaspoon olive oil

1 teaspoon salt

1 teaspoon garlic powder

1 small onion (chopped)

2 tablespoon margarine

1 teaspoon paprika

1 teaspoon fresh or dried rosemary

3 or 4 sweet potatoes (cut in half optional)

Wash the chicken and pat dry. Slice the lemon in half and squeeze the juice from one half over the chicken. Place the rind and one half of the chopped onion into the cavity.

In a small bowl mix the salt, garlic powder, paprika and rosemary and mix well. Rub the seasoning mix over the chicken.

Place the margarine under breast and over the chicken. Top with the remaining onion and drizzle with olive oil.

Place the chicken in a large roasting pan surrounded by the potatoes.

Bake at 400 degrees F for 1 and ½ to 2 hours until the chicken skin has become golden and crispy. As the chicken cooks spoon drippings over the potatoes every half hour.

When chicken is cooked, cut into the thigh joint. If the juices are clear, the chicken is cooked. The temperature on a meat thermometer should read 180 to 190 degrees.

Note:

Let it rest for about 8 minutes before carving.

If your timer has popped up, let the chicken continue to cook longer to obtain a crispy golden color.

68 Grilled Chicken
Frango no Churrasco

Frango Churrasco is popular for summer cookouts, family picnics and festivals. There are many restaurants called Churrasqueiras throughout Portugal and in Portuguese immigrant communities which sell only barbequed chickens on its menu.

There are many different recipes for this dish from using basic salt and pepper, to adding oregano and rosemary. My recipe combines the classic Portuguese spices of salt, pepper, garlic, paprika and piri piri sauce in white wine.

Serves 4-6

2 small fryer chickens (3 to 4 pounds each)

4 cloves garlic crushed

2 teaspoons salt

1 tablespoon paprika

½ cup white wine

Juice of half a lemon

2 tablespoons piri piri or any hot sauce

2 tablespoons olive oil

Marinade to brush on chicken:

2 tablespoons butter or margarine

½ cup white wine

Leftover marinade

Butterfly the chicken by cutting down the back bone and split it at the breast.

Mix the salt, pepper, garlic, paprika, wine lemon and piri piri sauce in a small bowl. Coat the chicken with the marinade. Place in a shallow pan or plastic bag and store in the refrigerator for at least 2 hours or best, if left overnight.

Remove the chicken from the refrigerator for at least 30 minutes before cooking on grill. When ready to cook, remove chickens from the pan and reserve marinade.

Place the chicken skin side up on the hot grill. Close the grill and let chicken cook for 10 minutes.

Check the chicken every 5 minutes keeping it away from flames.

In a small saucepan, mix any leftover marinade with the butter and ½ cup of wine and bring to a boil on stovetop grill and then place on grill to keep warm for basting the chicken.

Cook chicken for approximately 45 minutes to 1 hour. Baste with the leftover marinade every few minutes until cooked.

Note:

You may also finish cooking the chicken in the oven for 10 minutes at 350 degrees F if needed.

69 Oven Baked Piri Piri Chicken
Frango Piri Piri

Piri Piri Chicken comes out juicy and flavorful with a spicy kick When you can't cook outside on the grill during the cold months, cook this chicken under the oven broiler for 10 minutes and then finish it off it the oven.

Serves 4-8

2 small fryer chickens (about 3 pounds each)

2 teaspoons salt

1 teaspoon pepper

1 teaspoon garlic powder

1 teaspoon of paprika

2 tablespoons of piri piri or any hot sauce

¼ cup of Vinho Verde or white wine

Marinate the chickens with all the ingredients and leave them overnight in the refrigerator or for at least 2 hours before cooking.

Arrange the chickens on a large broiling or baking tray. Broil in your oven until the skin becomes golden brown for about 10 minutes.

Note: Leave the oven door slightly open.

Turn off broiler after 10 minutes and set the oven at 400 degrees F.

Place the chicken skin side up in the middle oven rack and cook for 1 hour or until the chicken is fully cooked and crispy.

Serve with more hot sauce for dipping if desired.

70 Portuguese Chicken with Rice
Arroz de Frango

My father disliked potatoes, so much, that my mother cooked rice many days of the week for our family dinners, including this chicken and rice dish. We had it so many times that my father often said; "We eat so much chicken that soon, we'll grow wings!" **Serves 4-6**

1 small fryer chicken 3-4 pounds (cut into about 10 pieces)

2 cups of long grain rice

1 small onion (chopped)

1 small garlic clove (chopped)

1 bay leaf

2 large carrots (chopped)

1 small very ripe tomato

¼ cup of olive oil

1 teaspoon paprika

1 tablespoon salt

1 pinch of black pepper

½ cup of white wine

1 chicken bouillon cube

5 cups of boiling water

Wash and pat dry the chicken and remove excess skin from the chicken if you desire. Marinate with the salt, pepper, paprika, wine, and let sit for at least 2 hours or overnight in the refrigerator.

When ready to cook, saute the onion and garlic in the olive oil in a heavy stove top casserole pan or deep skillet until translucent.

Add the chicken, carrots, tomato, and bay leaf. Cook on medium heat until the chicken browns, turning it over once in a while.

Add the wine, 2 cups water, bouillon, and any remaining marinade. Stir, cover and cook for at least 40 minutes.

After the 40 minutes add the 3 cups of boiling water, let it come to a boil and add the rice. Stir, wait for the rice to come to a boil, stir, cover, and cook on medium heat for about 15 minutes.

Remove from heat leaving covered until ready to serve.

71 Portuguese Style Roast Turkey
Peru Assado

Portuguese spices enhance the turkey in this recipe giving it a savory paprika flavor. There are many variations for preparing the Thanksgiving turkey but I learned this recipe when I was very young while watching my mother preparing the turkey the day before Thanksgiving the first year we arrived in America. **Serves 10-12**

1 (15) pound turkey

2 tablespoons of salt

1 lemon

1 large onion

1 large celery stalk

3 large sprigs of parsley

1 large carrot

¼ cup of olive oil

1 teaspoon garlic powder

1 tablespoon paprika

1 teaspoon pepper

2 tablespoon butter

½ cup of Vinho Verde or any white wine

3 celery stalks

1 large onion

Remove packaging and remove the neck and giblets from both cavities of the turkey.

Wash the turkey, the neck and giblets in very cold water. Reserve the neck and giblets for later use in stocks. Rub the inside and outside of the turkey evenly with the salt.

Slice the lemons in half and rub the inside and outside of the turkey with them, squeezing the juice as you rub. Place the rinds inside the cavity.

Spread the butter underneath the breast skin and on top of the turkey and coat with the paprika, pepper and garlic powder leaving a small amount to marinate the cavity.

Place the celery, onion and carrot inside the cavity. Rub the turkey with the olive oil. Place in the refrigerator and leave overnight to marinate.

Preheat oven to 350 degrees F.

Take the turkey out of the refrigerator at least 30 minutes before cooking. Place a few stalks of celery and a few slices of onion at the bottom of a large roasting pan that has a lid, and place turkey over them.

Note:

An average turkey of about 15 pounds will take about 3 hours to cook at 350 degrees.

Although your timer may pop up, it may not mean it's fully cooked, test the turkey with thermometer. It should reach 165 degrees F.

Marinate the turkey with the pan juices every hour.

If you like your turkey skin a dark golden color, remove the foil during the last 30 minutes of cooking.

Let the turkey sit at least 20 minutes before carving.

Do not discard the cooking juices. Save them to make homemade pan gravy.
Warm the turkey with a little bit of hot chicken or turkey broth.

Note: *A simple test to see if the turkey is cooked::*

Pull the thigh away from the body; if the thigh bone doesn't break off easy continue cooking the turkey longer.

Pan Gravy:

Create pan gravy by simply straining the juices, into a small saucepan. Let juices sit for a few minutes and remove any excess grease from the top.

Add few tablespoons of flour and cook for at least 5 minutes on low heat stirring constantly until the gravy is thick.

Add a little cream or milk to make lighter gravy.

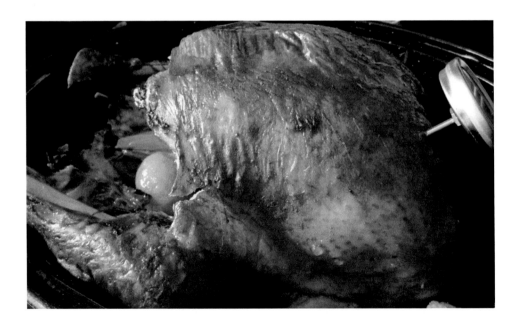

72 Braised Pork and Clams Alentejana Style
Carne de Porco à Alentejana

This traditional recipe is found on the menus of Portuguese restaurants throughout the world. The name, "Alentejana" means that the dish comes from the Alentejo region of Portugal. The origin of its name, "Além-Tejo", literally translates to "Beyond the Tagus" or "Across the Tagus". The region is separated from the rest of Portugal by the Tagus River and extends to the south where it borders the Algarve region.

The name Carne de Porco Alentejana was to distinguish that the pork used in the dish is from that region of the country which produces the Black Iberian Pig.

The meat from the Iberian pig has a higher fat content which produces a more tender and flavorful meat. My husband always says; "Just like Jell-O, there's always room for Carne Alentejana!" **Serves 6-8**

---

2 pounds boneless pork loin (cut into 2 in cubes)

1 small onion chopped

½ teaspoon cumin powder

2 cloves chopped garlic

1 teaspoon red pepper paste (optional)

1 and ½ teaspoons salt

2 pounds small fresh little neck clams

1 bay leaf

¼ cup olive oil

1 cup white wine or Vinho Verde

1 tablespoon smoked paprika

1 chicken bouillon cube

2 teaspoons piri piri or hot sauce

4 cups potatoes (cut in 2 inch cubes)

Oil for frying potatoes

Garnish Optional:

Olives

Chopped fresh cilantro

½ cup pickled Giardiniera vegetables

Season pork in a large bowl, with; salt, garlic, bay leaf, paprika, cumin, red pepper, and ½ cup of the wine. Stir well and let marinate for at least 2 hours or leave overnight in the refrigerator.

Before you begin cooking the pork, fry the potatoes in hot oil until golden brown, and season with salt. Set aside.

Place clams in a bowl with cold water and 1 tsp salt. Let pork sit for about ½ to 1 hour in refrigerator.

Remove pork from refrigerator 30 minutes before cooking.

Preheat large skillet or wok on high heat with ¼ cup olive oil. Add onions and cook for about 1 minute. Drain the pork saving the marinade, and add to the onions. Let meat brown on all sides for about 5 minutes.

Rinse and dry clams. Add to the pork along with the wine, and the leftover marinade. Cover and cook on medium heat until clams open for about 10 minutes. Add more wine and hot sauce if desired. When pork is cooked, add fried potatoes and stir gently on low heat to absorb flavors.

Add Garnish as desired and serve.

Note:

Do not overcook the pork or it will become dry.

73 Presunto Stuffed Pork Loin
Lombo de Porco Recheado com Presunto

Presunto and cheese filling add a salty, smoky flavor to the pork loin and the caramelized onions and port wine reduction bring sweetness to balance the saltiness of the presunto.

This is a special occasion dish that will leave your guests very happy. I serve this pork with roasted potatoes but it also pairs well with rice.

Serves 6-8

1 (3 or 4 pound) boneless pork loin

6 slices of presunto or prosciutto (diced)

1 cup spinach (finely chopped) optional

3 tablespoons of fresh parsley (minced)

2 cloves of garlic (minced)

3 slices of your favorite cheese

4 tablespoons of olive oil

½ cup of bread crumbs

½ teaspoon salt

1 teaspoon garlic powder

1 teaspoon paprika

Caramelized Onions ingredients:

1 large onion sliced

½ cup red wine

½ cup Vinho do Porto (Port wine)

2 tablespoons butter

Place the presunto, spinach, bread crumbs 2 tablespoons oil, parsley and garlic in a small bowl and toss well.

Gently butterfly the pork loin and spread out flat on a cutting board.

Spread the spinach stuffing mix evenly over the pork and gently roll the pork into a log shape. Tie with trussing thread or use long skewers to hold the pork together. Season the pork with the salt, garlic powder and paprika.

Place the rolled pork in a saute pan and brown evenly in the remaining 2 tablespoons of the olive oil. Remove from pan and place in a roasting pan.

Caramelized Onions:

In the same saute pan, cook the onions for 1 minute to brown. Add the red wine, port, and the butter. Continue cooking on medium heat until the wine is reduced by one half and thickened.

Cook Pork:

Poor the onion wine reduction over the pork loin. Cook pork at 350 degrees F for 45 minutes to 1 hour until the pork reaches 165 degrees.

Set aside to rest for 5 minutes before slicing.

74 Grilled Pork Strips with Onions and Peppers
Bifanas com Cebolada

Bifanas are as popular in Portugal as hamburgers are in America. They are served barbequed at picnics, sporting events, and festivals.. They are easy to prepare at home, by simply grilling them on a stove top skillet. They can be served with or without onions depending on your preference.

Serve them as a main dish with a side of rice or potatoes, or as the classic "bifana sandwich" pork strips on a Portuguese roll.

Serves 4-6

2 pounds boneless pork loin	Slice the pork loin into ½ inch slices. Place the slices between plastic wrap and pound with a meat mallet until the pork is ¼ inch thick.
1 teaspoon salt	
1 teaspoon paprika	This process will make the pork very tender.
½ teaspoon pepper	Season with the remaining ingredients and let the pork marinate for at least ½ hour before cooking but best if left overnight in the refrigerator.
1 teaspoon garlic powder or 3 crushed garlic cloves	
½ cup of white wine	Cook on an outdoor hot grill or in saute pan for about 3 to 4 minutes per side or until fully cooked.
1 or 2 tablespoons piri piri sauce (adjust to your taste preference)	Top with Caramelized onions.

Caramelized Onions and Peppers Recipe: This onion recipe is very versatile and can be served over pork, steak or fish.

2 medium onions	Saute the onions and peppers with olive oil until translucent and slightly browned.
2 large bell peppers (optional)	
3 tablespoons olive oil	Add the remaining ingredients and cook until the onions are a golden colored.
½ teaspoon garlic powder	
½ teaspoon salt	Set aside on low heat until ready to pour over the pork.
½ teaspoon pepper	
2 tablespoons white wine or white vinegar	

75 Roast Pork Loin with Onion and Garlic
Lombo de Porco Assado

It doesn't get more basic than using salt, pepper, paprika, garlic and olive oil when cooking meats. I've added onions to bring a sweet and savory flavor to this classic pork dish. If you're having a large party, use a whole pork loin and double the recipe ingredients. **Serves 6-8**

---

1 (4) pound boneless pork loin with fat on

1 tablespoon salt

6 cloves fresh garlic (chopped)

1 teaspoon paprika

1 teaspoon black pepper

1 large sliced onion

1 tablespoon olive oil

Season the pork with salt, garlic, paprika and pepper and let it marinate for at least 1 hour or overnight in the refrigerator.

When ready to cook, top with the olive oil and the sliced onion. Roast the pork for about 1 hour and 15 minutes at 350 degrees F. basting with onion sauce every 20 minutes.

Cook for another 15 minutes. Test for doneness using a thermometer. When the temperature reaches 155 degrees F, remove the roast from the oven and let sit for about 20 minutes before carving.

76 Trasmontana Style Pork and Bean Stew
Feijoada à Transmontana

Feijoada originated around the 14th century in the Northern region of Portugal. At that time, meat was scarce due to meats being supplied to feed the soldiers at war. The poor peasants began using every part of the pig as a staple in their diets along with beans and cabbage which were easily available. Generally, the dish is made with white beans but in the Tras os Montes region, red kidney beans are used.

This recipe is adapted from my brother John's recipe which was a favorite dish on the Matador's menu. It's a perfect crowd pleaser for a party. It pairs well with rice but be sure to have some crusty rolls to absorb the delicious sauce. **Serves 4-8**

2 pounds baby back ribs

1 chouriço sausage

1 pound blood sausage (if desired)

1 pound (presunto, smoked shoulder ham, and fresh pork belly cut into 2 inch strips)

1 small cabbage or savoy cabbage (chopped)

2 carrots sliced

2 large cloves garlic chopped

1 large onion finely chopped

¼ cup olive oil

2 bay leaves

1 tablespoon salt

1 teaspoon sweet paprika

1 teaspoon cumin powder

2 to 3 large 32 oz. cans cooked kidney beans

2 pounds pig hocks or knuckles and pig ears (if desired)

½ cup crushed tomatoes

The night before cooking:

Salt the ribs, and pork belly. Wash the knuckles in cold water, salt them, and store in fridge overnight to absorb the salt.

The next day:

Cook the pork knuckles in a large pot of unsalted water for at least 1 and ½ hours or until they're easy to cut apart. Reserve 2 cups of the broth for later.

Meanwhile, saute onions, garlic, and bay leaf in the olive oil for about 5 minutes.

Add ribs, pork belly and paprika. Let cook for about 5 minutes stirring so they don't stick to pan.

Add 2 cups of cooking liquid from the knuckles and let the ribs cook for another 20 minutes, stirring once in a while.

Add the rest of the meats (chouriço, presunto, ham, knuckles) chopped cabbage, carrots, and tomato sauce.

Stir gently and let cook for about 30 minutes. Add the kidney beans, (add blood sausage if desired), and cook for another 10 minutes.

Stir the pot gently so you don't break up the beans or the cabbage.

Serve with Portuguese rice and crusty bread.

Note:

The dish tastes even better the next day so don't be afraid if you have leftovers.

If you find the stew has thickened the next day, simply add a little boiling water or broth to thin out the sauce.

77 Tripe and White Bean Stew
Dobrada

Dobrada is often called "Tripas à moda do Porto" and originates from the city of Porto. During the fifteenth century the best cuts of meat were sent from the docks of the city to the troops who were at war in Africa leaving the lower quality cuts behind. Dishes like this one were created to utilize these meats. This regional dish has since become famous and the residents of the city often called "tripeiros".

I've adapted this family recipe over the years by adding baby back ribs which are my husband and son's favorite cut of pork.

Serves 8-10

3 (32 oz.) cans of white northern beans

1 pound of pork baby back ribs (cut in half to 3 or 4 inches)

1 pound or more of tripe

1 pound of pig feet (optional)

1 large chouriço sausage (cut into ¼ inch slices)

1 tablespoon salt

Pepper

1 large onion (minced)

¼ cup olive oil

4 cloves garlic (mined)

1 bay leaf

½ teaspoon of cumin

2 carrots (sliced)

1 cup white wine

1 cup of crushed tomatoes

1 to 2 cups of chicken broth

1 teaspoon paprika

Parsley for garnish

Day before cooking:

Wash the tripe and pig feet. Salt the tripe, pig feet, and ribs and let them sit in the refrigerator overnight.

When ready to prepare:

Cook the tripe and the pig feet in boiling water for at least 1and ½ to 2 hours until tender.

When cooked, remove the meats and cut the tripe into small 1 or 2 inch pieces and the pig feet into 2 inch pieces. Set aside saving 2 cups of the broth for later if needed.

Heat the olive oil in a large heavy pan. Add the onions, garlic, carrots, bay leaf, and cumin and saute for about 5 minutes.

Add the ribs and brown for about 10 minutes on low medium heat. Add the tomatoes, wine, and paprika and cook for 5 minutes.

Add the broth, tripe and pig feet, chouriço, and the beans and cook on low medium heat for about 30 minutes stirring often.

Taste and add more seasonings if desired. Garnish with parsley.

Serve over Portuguese rice with crusty bread.

Note:

You may need to add some of the reserved broth if you find the stew too thick.

Store in the refrigerator and add a little boiling water if it has thickened too much when serving the next day.

78 Braised Pork with Potatoes
Carne de Porco à Portuguesa

This recipe is adapted from the classic Carne à Alentejana. It uses no clams but the flavor is just as intense. **Serves 6-8**

2 pounds boneless pork loin (cut in 2 inch cubes)

2 pounds peeled potatoes (cut in 1 inch cubes)

1 small onion chopped

2 cloves chopped garlic

1 teaspoon salt

¼ cup olive oil

1 bay leaf

1 cup Vinho Verde or white wine

1 tablespoon smoked paprika

1 chicken bouillon cube

1 teaspoon corn starch

1 cup water

2 teaspoons piri piri or any hot sauce

Place pork into large bowl. Add salt, garlic, piri piri, olive oil, bay leaf and ½ cup of the wine. Stir well and let marinate for about one hour. Leave overnight if time allows.

When ready to cook the pork fry the potatoes until golden brown and set them aside.

Drain the pork and save marinade.

Preheat large skillet or wok on high heat with ½ cup olive oil. Add onions and cook for about 1 minute, then add pork. (Do not add any liquid yet).

Let meat brown on all sides and cook for about 5 minutes. Add bouillon, water, wine, marinade and more hot sauce if desired. Cook for about 5 minutes longer.

In small bowl mix ½ cup water with the corn starch and stir until the corn starch is dissolved. Add cornstarch to the pork and let cook for 5 minutes until the thickened.

Add potatoes to pork, stir and cook on low for about 2 minutes. Garnish with olives and cilantro if desired.

79 Portuguese Dry Rub Pork Spare Ribs
Costela de Porco Assada

These ribs come out juicy and tender with the meat falling off the bone. The simple spices of garlic, paprika, salt and pepper is the perfect combination so keep it simple. Serve with roast potatoes or rice. **Serves 6-8**

---

1 rack of pork ribs (3 to 4 pounds)

2 teaspoons salt

2 cloves garlic (chopped)

2 teaspoons paprika

1 teaspoon garlic powder

1 teaspoon cumin

1 teaspoon black pepper

¼ cup white wine

1 tablespoon piri piri or hot sauce (optional)

1 tablespoon olive oil

Place all seasonings except the wine in a small bowl and mix them well.

Rub the ribs with the white wine and garlic and let sit for a few minutes. Rub with seasoning mix and let sit for at least 2 hours but best if left overnight marinating in the refrigerator.

Take the ribs out of the refrigerator 30 minutes before cooking to reach room temperature and place them in a baking pan.

Drizzle ribs with the olive oil. Bake at 325 F for 2 hours, or until fully cooked, and the meat falls off the bone.

Note:

You may also cook these ribs on the outdoor grill. Cook them at medium heat turning them over every 5 to 10 minutes until they get golden brown.

Test the ribs by cutting through one rib. If the knife cuts easily through the rib, it will be done.

80 Roasted Pork Shoulder with Roasted Potatoes
Pernil Assado com Batatas

This pork shoulder recipe is simple to make on a lazy Sunday because you just put it in the oven and it cooks on its own. The pork comes out moist and flavorful. You'll have plenty of leftovers for the next day. Shred pork with a fork to make one of my family's favorite, pulled pork sandwiches on a crusty Portuguese roll.

Serves 10-12

1 (6 to 8 pound) fresh pork shoulder

2 tablespoons sea salt or kosher salt

1 teaspoon fresh ground pepper

3 garlic cloves (chopped)

1 large onion (chopped)

3 large carrots (cut into quarters)

1 bay leaf

6 to 8 potatoes (cut into cubes)

1 tablespoon olive oil

1 teaspoon paprika

1 cup of white wine

Note:

Let pork sit for at least 30 minutes to reach room temperature before prepping.

Preheat oven to 400 degrees F.

Wash and pat dry the shoulder. Place on a cutting board and score the skin being careful not to cut into the meat. Season the pork with salt. Place skin side up and place in large roasting pan with olive oil. Cook uncovered for 30 minutes until the skin starts to get crackling and browned.

After 30 minutes, turn the heat down to 325 degrees. Cover with the lid or very tightly with heavy foil and cook for 2 hours.

After 2 hours, remove the pan from the oven and coat the pork with the paprika, garlic and onions. Place the carrots in the pan evenly around the pork and baste with pan drippings. Add the wine and stir.

Cover the pork and continue cooking at 325 degrees for 1 hour. After 1 hour, baste with pan drippings.

Add the potatoes evenly around the pork and baste with drippings. Add a little more wine if you find the juices have dried out.

Cover and cook for another 45 minutes at 325 degrees.

Let pork rest for 10 minutes before slicing.

81 Steak and Egg Portuguese Style
Bife à Portuguesa

You'll find this classic steak dish on just about every Portuguese restaurant's menu. What makes this dish so flavorful is the combination of red wine, garlic and olive oil which creates a rich sauce that is poured over the steak and egg. **Serves 2**

2 (8oz) sirloin steaks (½ or 1 inch thick)

4 cloves garlic (sliced)

Salt

Pepper

2 eggs

1 tablespoon olive oil

4 or 6 small potatoes (peeled and sliced into ¼ inch slices or regular cuts)

Oil for frying potatoes

Wine reduction:

2 tablespoons olive oil

2 tablespoon of butter

½ cup red wine

Season the steaks with salt and pepper and let marinade overnight or for at least 1 hour.

Fry potatoes in hot oil, drain, and season with salt and keep warm in the oven.

Cook steaks with the garlic in hot skillet with 1 tablespoon olive oil for 3 minutes on each side. Remove from pan and add wine reduction ingredients. Cook the reduction until reduced by half.

Place the steaks back in the pan on low heat with the reduction.

Meanwhile, cook 2 eggs sunny side up in a separate small nonstick skillet.

Heat a large serving plate in the oven. Place steak in the center of the plate surrounded by the home fries.

Place one egg on top of each steak. Pour sauce from the pan over the steak and eggs. Season with more salt and pepper. Garnish with parsley if desired.

Note:

This dish is usually served with a serving of Portuguese rice as well but optional.

82 Spicy Beef Kabob Skewers
Espetada de Bife com Piri Piri

These beef kabobs are simple to make for a cook out. The sweet roasted onion and red pepper, tones down the spiciness in the piri piri. Serve over rice for a perfect combination.
Serves 4-6

2 pounds of sirloin or beef tenderloin (approximately 6 to 8 oz. per person)

1 large onion

1 large red or green pepper

1 teaspoon of salt

1 teaspoon pepper

2 cloves crushed garlic

1 teaspoon paprika

1 to 2 teaspoons piri piri or hot sauce

2 tablespoons olive oil

Butter or margarine

Skewers

Note:

Soak the wooden skewers in water for 30 minutes before making kebabs.

Cut the steak and vegetables into 2 inch cubes and season with the salt, pepper, garlic, 1 tablespoon olive oil and hot sauce.

Make the kabob by skewering the steak and vegetable in alternate rotation. Cover and let marinate for 1 to 2 hours in refrigerator.

When ready to cook, take the kabobs out of the refrigerator and let them sit for 10 minutes. Brush with the remaining olive oil.

Preheat the grill to medium-high heat and cook kebobs until browned about 8 to 10 minutes total cooking time or depending on your grill.

Place onto a warm tray. Brush with butter, and cover with aluminum foil. Let rest for 2 to 3 minutes.

83 Chouriço Omelet
Omelete de Chouriço

The humble chouriço omelet is very popular. It's delicious, simple to make, and perfect for breakfast, a quick lunch, or even dinner. The grilled chouriço gives the eggs a sweet and spicy paprika flavor. **Serves 2-4**

6 eggs

½ pound chouriço (sliced)

½ small onion (minced)

1 tablespoon parsley (minced)

1 tablespoon water

2 tablespoons olive oil

Salt

Pepper

1 small tomato (chopped) (optional)

Beat eggs in a large bowl with the water and season with salt and pepper.

Heat the oil in a large nonstick skillet on medium heat. Add the onion and saute until translucent. Add the chouriço, and cook on medium heat until slightly browned on each side.

Gently add the beaten eggs evenly over the chouriço.

Let the eggs cook while gently loosening the cooked eggs from the sides with a spatula allowing the uncooked eggs to seep to the sides. When the bottom of the omelet is browned, cover the pan with a flat plate large enough to cover the pan.

Flip the omelet over, uncooked side down and let cook for a few minutes longer.

Garnish with parsley, add salt and pepper.

Serve hot or cold.

dessert | sobremesa

Portugal's love of egg rich desserts began centuries ago. It is believed that the large use of eggs in their desserts was due to the process of Portuguese wineries using egg whites to clarify the wines. The wineries gave the many egg yolks that were left behind in this process to convents, which would make desserts to raise money for the poor in the community.

84 Portuguese Custard Tarts
Pastéis de Nata

These pastries are probably the favorite and most popular dessert. Once you try this recipe and experience just how easy they are to make at home, you'll never buy them at a bakery again.

Before we get started, I want to share with you the history of this famous pastry that was first created over 200 years ago.

Portuguese Egg Custard Tarts, famously known as Pastéis de Belem are famous in many countries all over the world. The original Pastéis de Belem, were first created at the Monastery of Jeronimos in Belem, Lisbon in 1837.

Casa Pasteis de Belem is located in the town of Belem in Lisbon, Portugal. The official name of the town is "Santa Maria de Belem" but it's referred to as "Belem". The name "Belem" originated from the Portuguese word for "Bethlehem".

Many bakeries have tried to replicate the recipe to no avail. The equally famous; "Pasteis de Nata" it's copycat version, has become a famous substitute for the original at every Portuguese bakery throughout Portugal and many other countries around the world.

The pastry's name was trademarked in 1911, which means the company is the only one that can call the famous sweets by that name.

I recommend that you try making this recipe a few times to adjust for your own oven temperature and baking time.

Makes approximately 20

1 pound defrosted puff pastry dough (your local bakery may sell it or find it in the freezer section of your grocery store)

2 cups whole milk (must be whole milk not low fat or skim)

1 and ½ cups sugar

½ cup flour

1 cup water

2 slices lemon peel

1 stick cinnamon

7 extra large egg yolks (room temp)

Cinnamon for garnish

Prepare muffin tins and dough:

Generously grease your muffins tins very well with margarine.

Tins should be Aluminum or Stainless. Do not use nonstick bakeware.

You can also use small bakeware ramekins. Puff pastry dough should be defrosted but very cold. Do not use warm dough.

Place your pastry dough on cutting board and roll to 1/8th inch thickness. Cut out diameter size circles to fit the bottoms of your muffin tins and up the sides.

Mold the pastry dough to form shells inside tins. I find that it's easier to cut out the round shape rather than mold individually.

If you find the dough is getting too warm, place in the refrigerator to cool for a few minutes

Prepare Syrup:

In a small pan, heat the water and sugar on medium heat stirring well.

Let the sugar water reach boiling point and let boil for 3 more minutes. Remove from heat, let cool.

Instructions Cream Filling:

Place ¾ cup of milk in a large bowl. Add flour and beat until smooth. Set aside.

Meanwhile, heat up the remaining milk with the lemon rind and cinnamon stick. When the milk reaches boiling point, add the milk and flour mixture and continue beating well until it reaches boiling point again. Set aside.

Let the milk and flour mixture cool completely in refrigerator for 10 minutes.

Add the sugar syrup to the milk mixture in a very fine drip while continuing beating until mixture is creamy smooth.

Pour the custard through a fine strainer to catch any lumps.

Strain the egg yolks through a fine metal strainer. Add the yolks to the cooled milk and beat well until smooth and creamy.
Pour the egg mix into the pastry lined tins or ramekins to about ¾ inches full.

Cooking:

Cook in a preheated oven at 485 degrees F for 20 to 25 minutes until the custard bubbles and turns golden brown.

Check your tarts after 15 minutes and every few minutes to be sure they do not burn. Let the tarts cool for about 10 to 15 minutes.

Note:

Let cool and sprinkle with cinnamon if desired before serving.

Tarts in Ramekins may take longer to cook.

Depending on your oven, you may not get a burned color on custard so you will have to cook longer.

85 Portuguese Sponge Cake
Pão de Lo

This light and fluffy cake is the most well-known and favorite cake in our cuisine. It is virtually fat free since it uses no oil, butter or fat in the recipe.

The cake was a big hit a few years ago during Christmas when I gave it as homemade gifts along with the recipe card, and the Bundt pan to cook it in.

Makes 1 cake - Serves 10-12

10 jumbo eggs (room temperature)

1 and ½ cups sugar

2 cups sifted flour

¼ teaspoon salt

1 teaspoon baking powder

1 teaspoon grated zest (optional)

Note:

I used a silk Poinsettia plant. Do not use real Poinsettia since they are poisonous.

Eggs should be at room temperature. Place cold eggs in a bowl of warm water for about 15 minutes before preparing recipe.

Aluminum pans work best for baking.

Use a large 12 cup Bundt pan.

In a large bowl beat the eggs until foamy. Add sugar and beat for at least 20 minutes until batter becomes very thick. Add lemon at this point if desired.

Note: Beat only 10 minutes if you use a Kitchenaid mixer until stiff peaks form.

While the eggs are beating, sift flour, salt and baking powder in a small bowl.

Add the flour mixture ¼ cup at a time on very low speed or fold in with a spatula. This process should only take about 3 to 5 minutes.

Grease and lightly flour a large tube pan and line the top rim with parchment paper. Gently pour the batter into the pan being careful not to deflate the batter..

Cook at 350 degrees F for 45 minutes or until a toothpick comes out clean.

Let the cake cool for about 10 minutes before removing it from the pan.

Remove parchment paper and place on serving dish.

86 Lemony Sweet Rice Pudding
Arroz Doce

Cinnamon was discovered in the early 1500's by Portuguese traders in Ceylon, known as; present-day Sri Lanka. Today, the spice is used in many of Portugal's egg rich desserts and in savory dishes as well. This rice pudding is made using milk, cinnamon and lemon zest.
Serves 8-10

3 cups whole milk (scalding)

3 egg yolks

1 cup rice (preferably short grain)

2 cups water

½ teaspoon salt

1 or 2 slices of lemon peel

1 cup granulated sugar

½ cinnamon stick

Powdered cinnamon

In a large heavy saucepan, bring the water, cinnamon stick, salt, and lemon peel to a boil.

Add rice, bring to a boil and cook on medium heat until all the water has evaporated.

Add the hot milk and cook for at least 25 minutes on low heat stirring once in a while. Add the sugar, stir and cook for 5 minutes longer and remove pan from heat.

Meanwhile beat egg yolks. Temper the eggs by adding a few tablespoons of the rice mixture to the eggs and mix well. Add the eggs to the rice and stir well in the pan.

Note:

Be sure the rice is not boiling but let the eggs cook in the hot rice for about 1 minute. Remove from heat.

Remove lemon peel and the cinnamon stick. Pour into a flat serving dish and decorate with powdered cinnamon.

87 Angel Hair Pasta Dessert
Aletria

This egg noodle dessert served at Christmas and special occasions is made with the same basic ingredients as the ever popular Arroz Doce, rice pudding. **Serves 8-10**

7 cups of whole milk

6 eggs

1 and ½ cups of sugar

1 teaspoon salt

1 cinnamon stick

2 slices of lemon peel

1 (12 oz.) package of very fine egg noodles

Pour milk, sugar, salt and cinnamon stick into a large pan and bring it to a boil, stirring constantly.

Meanwhile, beat the eggs in a small bowl and slowly blend some heated milk into the eggs and stir. Set aside.

Break up the noodles and add them to the boiling milk. Stir constantly until the noodles are cooked and remove from the heat.

Slowly add egg mixture into the cooked noodles and stir.

Remove the lemon peel and cinnamon stick.

Pour the mixture into a large serving platter and let cool completely.

Sprinkle or decorate with cinnamon and serve.

88 Fried Dough with Sugar and Cinnamon
Filhóses

Filhóses are made by stretching out the risen dough into sections and then frying them in hot oil. Many families have their own recipes and carry on the traditions of making this dessert with each generation. The pastry is very popular on holidays such as, Easter, Christmas, New Year's Day, and at many celebrations.

Makes approximately 3 dozen

9 cups all-purpose flour

1 cup sugar

1 and ½ teaspoon salt

6 eggs

1 stick butter or margarine (8 tbsp)

1 teaspoon lemon or orange zest

2 cups whole milk

¼ cup fresh orange juice

Oil to fry (corn oil or vegetable oil works best)

Ingredients to make the starter yeast:

3 tablespoons flour

½ teaspoon sugar

2 packages of dry yeast

½ cup warm water

First step:

Mix the ingredients in the starter yeast and set aside until bubbles form.

Second step:

Put the milk and butter in a pan on low heat until butter is melted.

In a large bowl, mix eggs, salt, sugar, lemon zest, and orange juice. Beat with electric mixer for 2minutes.

Add the milk and butter and mix for 30 seconds. Add yeast mix and flour and knead well until the dough is elastic and smooth.

Cover and let rest for 30 minutes. Punch down the dough, cover and let it rise until doubled.

In a deep fryer heat the oil to 375 degrees F.

Stretch pieces of the dough into thin strips of desired sizes of about 3 by 4 inches.

Fry until golden brown.

Drain on paper towels.

Dust with granulated sugar.

89 Portuguese Donuts with Sugar and Cinnamon
Sonhos

Sonhos are "dreams" in Portuguese. These little fried treats are similar to filhós, but no yeast is used in preparing the dough for frying. The flour is cooked in water, butter and eggs and then beaten to form a basic Choux paste often used for baking éclairs and cream puffs. The donut like puffs are lightly fried and then dipped in sugar and cinnamon while still warm.

Makes approximately 2 dozen

6 extra-large eggs

2 cups flour

¾ cup water

¾ cup milk

½ teaspoon salt

½ stick butter or margarine

1 slice lemon peel

Sugar and cinnamon for topping

Ina large heavy pan, place the water, milk, butter, lemon rind, and salt over medium heat and bring to boiling point.

Stir in flour with a wooden spoon until the flour forms soft dough. A ball shape will be formed and separate from the sides of the pan.

Remove the dough from heat and place into a medium bowl. Let the dough cool for a few minutes.

Beat in eggs one a time creating a smooth batter.

Heat the oil to 365 degrees F.

Shape the dough into round doughnuts using a large tablespoon. Fry 4 or 5 pieces at time, until golden brown. Pierce the sonhos slightly as they cook. Keep the heat at a steady temperature.

Drain on paper towels. Sprinkle sugar and cinnamon while still hot

90 Cavacas Pastry with Sugar Icing
Cavacas

This Portuguese popover dessert cooks to a light and airy texture with a lemony sugary glaze over the top. The origin is not known but it's a very popular dessert

Makes approximately 1 dozen

8 extra-large eggs (room temperature)

¾ cup olive oil

2 cups sifted all-purpose flour

Pinch of salt

1 cup olive oil for coating tins

Cooking spray

Icing:

1 cup confectioner's sugar

2 to 3 tablespoons milk

1 teaspoon grated lemon zest

Sift together the salt and flour and set aside.

In a large mixing bowl beat the eggs and olive oil for a few minutes. Add the flour mixture and beat for at least 15 to 20 minutes until the batter has reached a smooth consistency.

Grease popover or large muffin tins with cooking spray and a little olive oil.

Fill each cup one half to top with batter.

Cook at 350 degrees F for 50 minutes. Do not open the oven or the cavacas will collapse!

Gently remove from oven. Let the popovers cool a few minutes in pan before removing.

Make the icing by combining the confectioners' sugar and the lemon zest with milk until it reaches a smooth consistency. Taste and add more lemon zest if you prefer.

Drizzle with icing.

91 Lemony Cake Roll
Torta de Limao

This lemony light cake roll adapted from my sister Rose's recipe. She's the official "Torta" maker for our family gatherings. You can be creative with this recipe, so go ahead and substitute the lemon filling with your favorite sauces, such as; chocolate, marmalade, fresh berries or jarred fruit fillings.

Makes 1 - Serves 6-8

5 eggs separated and room temperature

¾ cup flour

1 teaspoon baking powder

½ teaspoon salt

2 teaspoon crated lemon peel

1 tablespoon lemon juice

1 package instant Vanilla or Lemon pudding mix

1 and ½ cups milk

¾ cup sugar

Preheat oven to 350 degrees F. Grease or spray a large sheet pan and line with parchment paper.
Combine flour, salt, and baking powder in a bowl.

In a separate large bowl beat egg yolks with ¼ cup of sugar until lemony. Add flour mix, lemon zest and lemon juice and mix well for about 5 minutes. Set aside.

In a separate bowl beat the egg whites until they form soft peaks. Add the ½ cup sugar gently into the whites until stiff peaks form.

Gently fold the egg whites into the egg yolks. Pour the mixture into the lined sheet pan spreading evenly. Cook for about 15 minutes or less depending on your oven. The cake should be golden light brown in color.

While the cake bakes, prepare the pudding using only 1 and ½ cups of milk and set aside.

Place a clean linen white kitchen towel or parchment paper on the counter and sprinkle generously with granulated sugar. Slowly flip the cooked cake pan onto the towel. Peel off the parchment paper, then roll up the cake with the dish towel and let it sit for 5 minutes for the cake to cool.

Unwrap the cake gently. Spread the pudding evenly over the cake. Remove towel and gently roll the cake into a log shape. Place with edges side down on serving dish.

Sprinkle top with a dusting of sugar.

92 Lemony Rice Flour Cupcakes
Bolos de Arroz

These very popular rice flour cakes are light and lemony sweet, and they're found in every Portuguese bakery. My first memory of eating Bolos de Arroz was when my family traveled back to Portugal for a summer vacation when I was twelve years old. The morning after arriving in Lisbon, my parents took my brothers, sisters and I downstairs to eat breakfast at the bakery located in my Aunt's apartment building. When I stepped onto the sidewalk, the aroma of the fresh bread baking that morning made my mouth water. After eating these rice flour cakes, that day, they became one my favorite pastries. **Makes 6 large or 12 mini cakes**

1 and ½ cups of sugar

2 cups flour

1 cup rice flour

¾ cup of margarine

2 tablespoons of baking powder

6 eggs (room temperature)

1 cup of warm milk

2 teaspoons of grated lemon zest

Sugar for dusting cupcakes

Make cake liners by cutting parchment paper in strips long enough to fit inside of popover pans or large muffin tins leaving a 1 inch overlap on top.

Beat together the sugar and margarine until light and fluffy.

Add the lemon zest and beat well.

In a separate bowl, beat the eggs and milk until well incorporated, add to the sugar mix, and beat the batter for at least 5 minutes.

Add both flours and baking powder to the batter and beat for at least 5 minutes or until the batter is light yellow, and fluffy.

Fill cups ¾ inches to top.

Cook at 350 degrees F for 20 to 30 minutes or until a toothpick comes out clean.

During the last 5 minutes of cooking, sprinkle tops with granulated sugar and cook until golden brown.

You can also make mini cakes in your muffin tins. Line with cupcake liners, fill and bake for only 15 minutes.

93 Caramel Flan
Pudim Flan

Caramel Flan is quite easy to make despite its appearance. It's a perfect dessert to impress your guests on special occasions. The first time I ate flan was when I was twelve years old while vacationing in Portugal with my parents and siblings. It's one my favorite desserts which I make on every special occasion.

Be sure to only use whole milk in this recipe to create a smooth creamy textured flan.

Serves 8-12

6 large eggs (room temperature)

3 cups whole milk

1 cup sugar

¼ teaspoon salt

1 teaspoon (vanilla, anisette liquor, or caramel glaze) this is optional

Whipped cream (optional for serving)

Candy sugar pearls (optional for garnish)

Caramel glaze ingredients:

1 cup sugar

Note: Use eggs at room temperature:

Take your eggs out of the refrigerator to get them to room temperature or place them in a bowl of lukewarm water for about 20 minutes.

Prepare caramel glaze first:

Place the sugar in a large heavy skillet. Cook on medium heat until the sugar melts and begins to turn caramel colored and thick like syrup while stirring occasionally.

This will take probably 5 to 8 minutes depending on your burners. If the sugar is hardening too quickly, just drizzle a little water around the edges of the pan into the sugar.

Take the pan off the heat and let it rest for one minute.

Caution the sugar is hot! Do not touch.

It's very hot! If you smell a burning aroma it means you've cooked the sugar too long and burned it. You must start over again.

Coat the pan for baking flan:

Pour the hot caramel into a medium soufflé dish or bundt pan. Reserve 1 teaspoon.

Swirl the pan to coat the bottom and 1 inch up the sides with the caramel.

Let the Caramel harden and put the pan aside while you make the flan.

Prepare custard:

In a medium bowl, beat the eggs with 1 cup of sugar until lemony colored.

Meanwhile, heat the milk until scalding but not boiling. Let the milk cool down and then add ¼ cup of milk, to the beaten eggs while continuing to beat on low. If the milk is too hot, you'll discover that you just made scrambled eggs.

Continue beating on low and slowly add the rest of the milk 1 cup at a time until all of the milk is incorporated. Add vanilla, anisette, or reserved caramel.

Pour into the soufflé dish.

Place dish into a larger oven proof deep dish pan. Pour enough water into the large pan to reach up to 1 inch of the soufflé dish.

Cook:

Cook at 350 degrees F for 60 to75 minutes or until a toothpick comes out clean

Let the flan cool and place it still in its pan in the refrigerator overnight.

When ready to serve, loosen the sides of the flan with a knife and shake the pan slightly to loosen.

Cover the top of the flan with a deep serving dish and invert it holding the dish tightly onto a serving dish.

Spoon out the caramel left in the bottom of the cooking dish over the flan.

If the caramel is too hard, simply soak the bottom of the pan in warm water to melt the caramel on the bottom.

Serve as is or with whipped cream and sugar pearls if desired.

94 Molotof Pudding
Pudim Molotof

This egg white soufflé dessert is light, airy and delicious. I will always remember the Portuguese chef named Miazette, at my brother's restaurant that taught me this recipe.
Serves 8-10

---

12 egg whites (room temperature)

2 cups sugar

Ingredients for caramel sauce:

2 cups sugar

1 tablespoon water

Make Caramel glaze first:

Cook sugar in heavy saucepan with the water until it turns golden caramel brown.

If you smell smoke, you have burned the sugar and you must start over.

Put the caramel sauce into the bunt pan and reserve 3 tablespoons for adding to the egg whites later. Rotate the bottom of pan and sides to coat with caramel. Set aside.

Beat egg whites until stiff peaks form. Add sugar and beat gently to incorporate. Add the 3 tablespoons of reserved caramel. Beat slowly until the sugar is incorporated.

Gently place egg whites into bunt pan. Tap the pan gently a few times to remove any air bubbles.

Cook in the bain Marie water bath for 12 minutes at 375 degrees F.

Leave pan in oven and do not open oven for at least 10 minutes.

Remove from oven and let the soufflé cool before placing in refrigerator overnight.

When ready to serve, cover with a large serving platter and flip the soufflé bottom side up.

Spread any remaining caramel glaze from the pan over the soufflé and serve.

95 Aniz Flavored Tea Biscuits
Biscoitos com Aniz

These biscuit cookies are perfect for your afternoon tea or any time of the day. I add lemon zest or anisette liquor but you can leave it out completely. The biscuits store well in a cookie jar and freeze well, so cook up a double batch to enjoy later. We make these every Christmas and decorate them as wreaths and candy canes.

Makes approximately 2 dozen

3 cups flour plus more if needed

1 cup sugar

3 eggs (room temp)

6 tablespoons margarine or butter

2 teaspoons baking powder

1 teaspoon grated lemon zest or Aniz liquor (optional)

Preheat the oven to 350 degrees F.

Soften the butter and mix with sugar in a medium bowl until light and fluffy. Add the eggs and lemon and beat for about 1 minute.

Add the flour and baking soda to the sugar and mix with a dough hook for about 3 minutes until the batter forms into a ball.

Place the smooth dough onto a lightly floured cutting board and shape into a flat disc with ½ inch in height.

Cut the dough evenly into ½ inch by 5 inch strips. Roll each strip into a round snake like form, infinity shape, wreaths or letters.

Slightly grease a cookie sheet and place the biscuits evenly on the pan.

Cook for about 15 to 18 minutes or until slightly golden brown.

Store in cookie jars or food safe plastic bags.

96 Minho Style Honey Wine Toast
Rabanadas do Minho

Rabanadas do Minho are French toast covered in a red wine honey sauce. You may omit the wine honey sauce if you prefer a plain version. This recipe is easy and a great way to use up any of your leftover crusty bread.

When I was a little girl, I would wake up on Christmas Eve mornings smelling the aroma of the sugar and cinnamon sprinkled on the warm toast that my mother had just made for our Christmas Eve dessert table.

Serves 4-6

1 loaf of day old crusty Portuguese bread

2 cups milk

3 large eggs

1 tablespoon sugar

1 teaspoon cinnamon

Margarine for cooking

Sugar and cinnamon for topping

Red Wine Honey Sauce:

5 glasses wine

1 cup honey

1 teaspoon of cinnamon

Red Wine Honey Sauce Preparation:

Cook the wine, honey, and cinnamon in a saucepan until it comes to a boil. Cook for a few minutes until the wine reduces slightly.

Toast Preparation:

Slice the bread into 1inch slices and place in a deep dish pan.

Beat all the other ingredients in a bowl and pour evenly over bread. Let the bread slices sit in the egg for about 30 seconds and flip them over to absorb egg on the other side. Keep flipping the bread until all of the egg mixture is absorbed.

Meanwhile on medium high heat, melt margarine in a large flat skillet or griddle.

When the skillet is hot, lower the heat to medium and gently place the slices of bread on the grill greasing the pan as needed.

Cook both sides of the bread until golden brown and it becomes firm to the touch. If you find the bread still soggy, continue cooking them on low heat for longer.

Soak with honey wine sauce recipe if desired or simple sprinkle with sugar and cinnamon while still hot.

97 Maria Cookies Parfait
Bolo de Bolacha Maria

This easy recipe requires no baking and makes an elegant dessert. Bolo de Bolacha Maria is traditionally made with butter, or sweetened condensed milk, but my version uses homemade pastry cream which makes it lighter and uses less sugar. You'll find that you have all the ingredients for this recipe in your pantry. If you don't have Portuguese Maria Cookies, you can use the Mexican Maria cookies found in most grocery stores. **Serves 4-6**

---

1 package of Bolacha Maria (Maria cookies any brand)

1 or 2 cups of warm, strong, black coffee

2 cups of whole milk

3 large egg yolks

½ cup of sugar

¼ cup of corn starch

½ teaspoon of vanilla extract

2 tablespoons of butter

Pinch of salt

Whipped cream

Instructions for Pastry Cream:

In a small saucepan heat the milk, 1/4 cup of the sugar, vanilla and pinch of salt until scalding but not boiling and set aside.

Meanwhile mix the egg yolks with the remaining sugar and corn starch until smooth and creamy.

Slowly add the yolks to the milk beating as you pour.

Cook the milk mixture on medium heat for two minutes until it thickens stirring constantly and pour it into a bowl. Add the butter. Beat with a mixer for about 5 minutes until very smooth and creamy.

Cover the bowl and place in the refrigerator for at least 2 hours to cool completely and thicken.

Assemble the parfait:

Dip 1 cookie into the coffee for about 5 seconds and place into the bottom of parfait glass.

Spread 1 tablespoon of the pastry cream on top of the cookie. Continue layering at least 4 cookies alternating with the pastry cream.

At this point you can cover with plastic wrap and store in the refrigerator until ready to serve.

Top with whipped cream and sprinkle with crushed Maria cookies.

Note:

You can also make this recipe in a shallow glass serving bowl instead of individual parfaits but don't top with the whipped cream until ready to serve.

98 Fruit Salad with Port Wine

Salada de Fruta com Vinho do Porto

The strawberries and port wine combination in this recipe creates a sweet syrup that infuses the fruit. It's even better the next day so go ahead and make it ahead of time for your party.

I've been making this family favorite recipe which is my late mother in laws, for all of our family celebrations. If serving to children, just omit the port wine, it's just as good.

Serves 10-12

---

1 cup Vinho do Porto (Port wine)

2 cups fresh strawberries (cut into slices)

1 container frozen strawberries in syrup (defrosted)

1 can of pineapple chunks

1 can of sliced peaches

1 can of fruit cocktail

1 can of sliced peaches

1 can of sliced pear

1 cup grapes (optional)

Place all ingredients into a large bowl. Stir gently to incorporate the wine into the fruit.

Note:

You can also serve the salad immediately but it's best if left overnight in your refrigerator to allow the port wine to infuse into the fruit.

Store in the refrigerator for up to 3 days.

99 Creamy Custard with Caramelized Sugar
Leite Crème

The first time I ate this creamy stove top custard was when I was twelve years old while vacationing with my parents and siblings in Coimbra, Portugal. My Aunt made it for us as a snack after our long 4 hour taxi drive from Lisbon.

Serves 4-6

2 tablespoons corn starch

5 tablespoons sugar

3 egg yolks

2 cups whole milk

½ stick of cinnamon

1 slice lemon peel

In a medium bowl, beat the eggs and the milk with a whisk until well incorporated. Add the corn flour and sugar and mix well.

Add the lemon peel and cinnamon stick and heat in a saucepan on low medium heat stirring continuously.

Do not let the custard boil. If it begins to boil remove from heat to cool down while stirring. It should be thick enough to coat the spoon like pudding.

Pour into a serving platter or individual ramekins and let cool to room temperature.

Top with granulated sugar and place under broiler for a few minutes until the sugar is caramelized.

Sprinkle with cinnamon if desired.

100 Chocolate Roll
Torta de Chocolate

This cake roll is simple to make and takes less than 30 minutes to prepare. Your chocolate loving friends will love this cake and love you for making it for them. **Serves 6-8**

5 room temp eggs (separated)

¾ cup flour

1 teaspoon baking powder

¾ cups sugar

¼ teaspoon salt

1 cup chocolate spread

Preparation:

Preheat oven to 350 degrees F.

Grease or spray a large sheet pan and line with parchment paper.

Combine flour, salt, and baking powder in a bowl.

In a separate large bowl beat egg yolks with ¼ cup of sugar until lemony. Add flour mix, lemon zest and lemon juice and mix well for about 5 minutes. Set aside.

In a separate bowl beat the egg whites until they form soft peaks. Add the ½ cup sugar gently into the whites until stiff peaks form. Gently fold the egg whites into the eggs. Pour the mixture into the lined sheet pan spreading evenly. Cook for about 15 minutes or less depending on your oven. The cake should be golden light brown in color.

While the cake bakes, prepare the pudding using only 1and ½ cups of milk and set aside.

Place a clean linen white kitchen towel or parchment paper on the counter and sprinkle generously with granulated sugar.

Slowly flip the cooked cake pan onto the towel. Peel off the parchment paper, then roll up the cake with the dish towel and let it sit for 5 minutes for the cake to cool.

Unroll the cake gently. Spread the chocolate sauce evenly over the cake. Remove towel and gently roll the cake into a log shape.

Sprinkle top with a dusting of sugar.

101 Chocolate Flan Cake
Bolo de Chocolate e Pudim Flan

You won't believe the magic that happens when you make this chocolate flan cake. It's like having two desserts; chocolate cake and caramel flan all in one bite! This cake has Spanish origins but it has become very popular throughout the Portuguese community.

Serves 10-12

Chocolate Cake Ingredients:

1 Package of Devil's Food chocolate cake mix

3 eggs

1 cup water

1/3 cup vegetable oil

1 cup of any caramel sauce
(or make caramel sauce on this recipe)

Flan Ingredients:

1 (14 oz.) can sweetened condensed milk

1 (12 oz.) can evaporated milk

½ cup half and half

1 teaspoon of Aniz (Anise liquor) or 1 teaspoon vanilla

4 large eggs

Caramel Sauce ingredients:

1 and ½ cups sugar

Prepare Caramel Sauce First:

Place 1 and ½ cup sugar in a heavy skillet. Cook until the sugar dissolves and cooks to a dark caramel color. *Caution the sugar is very hot. Do not touch.* If the sugar begins to smoke it means you have burned the sugar. Discard and start over.

Prepare cake:

Preheat oven to 350 degrees F.

Heavily grease a large 12 cup bunt pan with cooking spray or margarine.

Pour the caramel evenly in bottom of the pan and shake pan to coat about 1 inch up the sides.

Prepare the cake by beating cake mix, water, oil and 3 eggs with electric mixer for about 3 minutes on medium speed and set aside.

Prepare the flan by mixing all the ingredients in a in a mixer at high speed for about 45 seconds.

Pour the cake batter into the Bundt pan. Slowly pour the flan mixture on top of the chocolate batter.

Note:

Don't worry that something may not seem right since the flan mixture will be very runny over the chocolate batter.

Cover the cake with heavy foil that has been coated with cooking spray and place in a deep roasting pan big enough to hold the cake in 2 inches of water in bain marie.

Bake the cake for about 1 hour and 10 minutes. Place the cake on the counter and let it cool for at least 2 hours.

When the cake is completely cooled, gently loosen the sides with a thin knife.

Place a large serving platter over the pan. Firmly hold the plate over the pan and carefully invert the cake. The cake will come out with the chocolate cake on the bottom and flan on the top.

Pour any remaining caramel from the pan over the flan.

Note:

To serve the cake the next day, place covered, unmolded cake in the refrigerator overnight and invert the next day.

Top with whipped cream and the remaining caramel sauce before serving if desired.

You can substitute homemade caramel sauce with jarred store bought caramel sauce.

index

about the authors

Maria Dias was born in Portugal and migrated to the United States as a young girl. She is a self-taught Cook/Blogger with over 25 years of experience in the food industry. Currently, she writes and prepares recipes for Tia Maria's Blog and writes for Portuguesediner.com. Her 100 Portuguese recipes from Tia Maria's Blog are currently available in Microsoft's Food & Drink App for PC and Mobile devices.

She has appeared on a local television station WWLP TV, cooking her recipes and has been featured in various media outlets both in the United States and in Portugal. She has also written food articles in Western Mass Women's Magazine and has also presented an online seminar "How to Start Your Own Food Blog" via the United States State Department in Brasilia Brazil.

Lisa Dias, Maria's daughter, creates recipes, maintains the website, and is the Illustrator/Photographer for Tia Maria's Blog and Portuguesediner.com

Maria and Lisa reside in Western Massachusetts where they continue their commitment of promoting and preserving Portuguese cuisine for the next generation and they are currently working on their second cook book.

Get more recipes and updates online at these websites:

Tia Maria's Blog

http://portuguesediner.com/tiamaria/

Tia Maria's Blog on Facebook

https://www.facebook.com/pages/Tia-Marias-Blog/463406760067

Tia Maria's Blog on Pinterest

https://www.pinterest.com/tiamariasblog/tia-maria-s-blog/